Report...

Idaho. Dept. of Finance, Idaho. Bank Commissioner, Idaho. Bureau of Banking

State of Idaho

BUREAU OF BANKING

His excellency, D. W. DAVIS, Governor,
　　　　State of Idaho, Boise, Idaho.

SIR:—

Agreeable to Section 5206 of Chapter 205 of the 1919 Compiled Laws of the State of Idaho, I have the honor to herewith submit for your consideration my report for the year ending December 31, 1920, which contains the following schedules, to-wit:

　　1.　Comparative Statement.

　　2.　Receipts and expenditures for the year and biennial appropriation.

　　3.　Banks chartered, nationalized, increasing capital stock, changing name and location, consolidated and closed.

　　4.　List of State Bank members of the Federal Reserve System.

　　5.　Reports of banks and trust companies as shown by call reports of November 15, 1920.

During the year five reports were asked for and made to this Department, on the same dates reports were made by national banks to the Comptroller of the Currency, namely, February 28, May 4, June 30, September 8, and November 15, 1920.

During the year five state banks were organized and authorized to do business by this Department, there was one nationalization, three banks were closed by the Department and one was consolidated. Two hundred thirty-two examinations were made; for these services fees were collected amounting to $11,620.91.

While the comparative statement shows a decrease in deposits of $13,-621,807.83, or a loss of 23.6 per cent, this decrease is only in a reasonable proportion to the general decrease throughout the country. In fact Idaho has not suffered proportionately in this respect to some of her sister states.

On September 27th Chief Examiner, H. G. A. Winter and myself examined the Commercial and Savings Bank of Mountain Home. The examination disclosed such a serious state of affairs that the bank was not opened for business the following day. At the time of closing the deposit liability was approximately $178,000.

Mr. Chas. H. Stewart of Mountain Home was appointed Special Deputy in Charge and on December 23, 1920, payment in full to the depositors was made.

On October 13, 1920, the deposit liability of approximately $500,000 of the Stockgrowers Bank and Trust Company of Pocatello was assumed by the National Bank of Idaho of that city. Mr. G. D. McClintock of Pocatello was appointed Special Deputy in Charge of the affairs of this Bank.

On November 3, 1920, the Coeur d'Alene Bank and Trust Company of Coeur d'Alene, Idaho, was taken in charge by Chief Examiner, H. G. A. Winter. The deposit liability of this bank is approximately $300,000. Mr. Ezra R. Whitla of Coeur d'Alene was appointed Special Deputy to take charge of the affairs of the bank. A ten per cent dividend has been paid to the depositors and it is expected to pay another dividend of ten per cent some time during January, 1921. Some loss to the depositors will result from this failure.

On November 29, 1920, the Grangeville Savings and Trust Company of Grangeville closed its doors with deposit liability of approximately $120,000. The closing of this bank was brought about by a depletion of its reserve and inability to secure funds soon enough to meet demands. Examination of this bank indicates it will be able to pay its depositors as soon as its affairs can be liquidated. Mr. G. W. Suppeger of Moscow was appointed Special Deputy to take charge of the affairs of this bank. Plans for reorganization are now being considered.

With few exceptions I have found the officers and directors of the banks under my jurisdiction ready and willing at all times to co-operate to the best of their ability with the Bureau of Banking.

I wish to express at this time my appreciation of the co-operation and support acorded me by the bankers of this State and the empoyees of this Bureau.

Respectfully submitted,

JOHN G. FRALICK,
Commissioner.

INNING WITH 1906.

	Nov. 20, '17 137 Banks	Nov. 1, '18 137 Banks	Nov. 17, '19 137 Banks	Resources	Nov. 15, '20 138 Banks
2.71	$31,019,629.52	$32,727,810.77	$41,773,562.65	Cash on hand	$ 1,528,199.03
5.00	78,718.99	102,238.69	134,841.85	Due from banks	7,203,504.69
				Checks and drafts	506,413.43
.98	3,684,945.84	6,400,773.18	8,949,979.08	Cash items	194,639.71
.15	1,644.71	3,969.69	5,252.49	Loans and Discounts	44,643,873.74
.54	1,359,237.69	1,453,773.09	1,562,986.86	Overdrafts	118,368.82
.26	437,855.48	446,864.47	491,375.50	Stocks, Bonds and Warrants ..	7,702,368.85
.38	11,686,308.55	8,717,731.48	13,688,629.40	Federal Reserve stock	83,100.00
.30	145,975.00	113,091.81	210,325.20	Premium on bonds	8,589.66
.58	578,978.49	395,487.63	664,431.78	Claims and Judgments	49,848.68
.94	1,965,173.88	1,594,489.61	1,785,268.77	Banking House, Furn. & Fixt.	1,607,072.70
.20	68,002.94	370,516.96	82,185.52	Other Real Estate	514,352.86
		39,000.00	55,650.00	Other Resources	94,944.24
				Expenses in excess of earn'gs	24,953.66
.04	$51,026,471.09	$52,365,746.18	$69,404,489.10	Total	$64,334,446.81

RECEIPTS.

Examination fees, 232 Examinations, 1920	$11,620.91
Charter Fees, 5 charters, 1920	125.00
Expenses refunded from defunct bank	342.38

Total receipts from Jan. 1, 1920, to Dec. 31, 1920 ....$12,188.29

EXPENDITURES.

Salary of Commissioner for 1920	$3,600.00	
Salary of Chief Deputy for 1920	2,700.00	
Salary of Deputies for 1920	1,666.70	
Salary of Chief Clerk and Stenographer, 1920	1,428.00	9,394.70

Traveling and Office Expense for 1920:

Railroad and Stage Fare	$1,110.16	
Hotel Expense	1,589.70	
Postage	144.72	
Telephone and Telegraph	359.96	
Printing and Stationery	315.25	
Office Supplies	187.14	
Premium on Bonds	85.57	
Sundries	46.87	2,839.37

Total expenditures from Jan. 1, 1920, to Dec. 31, 1920		$13,234.07
Biennial appropriation for salaries	$20,000.00	
Less Transfer to General Expense	1,400.00	18,600.00
Biennial appropriation for general expense	6,545.00	
Plus transfer from salaries	1,400.00	7,945.00

Total Biennial Appropriation	$26,545.00
Total expenses for Biennium	26,239.10

Balance of Biennial appropriation ....$ 305.90

DETAILED STATEMENT OF MONEY RECEIVED

First State Bank, Donnelly	$ 35.00
Intermountain State Bank, Cascade	35.00
First Bank of Homedale, Homedale (charter fee)	30.00
Bank of Commerce, Burley	77.50
Declo State Bank, Declo	43.50
Heyburn State Bank, Heyburn	40.00
Paul State Bank, Paul	40.00
Hazelton State Bank, Hazelton	43.50
Eden State Bank, Eden	40.00
Idaho State Bank, Twin Falls	60.00
Citizens State Bank, Buhl	80.00
Bank of Rogerson, Rogerson	46.00
Bank of Hollister, Hollister	43.50
Twin Falls Bank & Trust Co., Twin Falls	92.50
Burley State Bank, Burley	67.50
D. L. Evans & Co., Albion	43.50
Bank of Hansen, Hansen	46.00
Oakley State Bank, Oakley	51.00
Commercial & Savings Bank, Mountainhome	57.50
Grand View State Bank, Grand View	40.00
Bruneau State Bank, Bruneau	46.00
Bank of Kimberly, Kimberly	51.00

Bank of Murtaugh, Murtaugh	38.50
Farmers & Merchants Bank, Filer	43.50
Farmers Commercial & Savings Bank, Oakley	51.00
Bellevue State Bank, Bellevue	51.00
Picabo State Bank, Picabo	43.50
First State Bank, Richfield	43.50
Carey State Bank, Carey	50.00
Bank of Castleford, Castleford (charter fee)	30.00
Farmers & Merchans Bank, Rupert	43.50
First State Bank, Rockland	35.00
Evans State Bank, American Falls	51.00
Citizens State Bank, Gooding	51.00
Kuna State Bank, Kuna	43.50
Meridian State Bank, Meridian	43.50
Bank of Eage, Eagle	43.50
Middleton State Bank, Middleton	40.00
The Farmers Bank, Star	46.00
Declo State Bank, Declo	80.00
Bank of Soda Springs, Soda Springs	46.00
First Savings Bank, Pocatello	57.50
Commercial Bank, Shelley	51.00
Largilliere & Company, Soda Springs	51.00
Bank of Roberts, Roberts	40.00
Rexburg State Bank, Rexburg	70.00
Anderson Bros. Bank, Rigby	46.00
Fremont County Bank, Sugar City	46.00
Butte County Bank, Arco	38.50
Bank of Commerce, Arco	60.00
W. G. Jenkins & Co., Mackay	60.00
The Peoples Bank, Cambridge	52.50
First Bank of Council, Council	46.00
Meadows Valley Bank, New Meadows	43.50
Citizens Bank, Pocatelo	85.00
Culdesac State Bank, Culdesac (charter fee)	30.00
Blackfoot City Bank, Blackfoot	60.00
Ft. Lapwai State Bank, Lapwai	38.50
Idaho Trust Company, Lewiston	50.00
The Farmers Bank, Kendrick	40.00
Kendrick State Bank, Kendrick	42.50
Farmers Bank, Nezperce	43.50
Bank of Stites, Stites	28.50
State Bank of Kooskia, Kooskia	42.50
State Bank of Kamiah, Kamiah	51.00
Ilo State Bank, Craigmont	51.00
Bank of Vollmer, Craigmont	42.50
Bank of Reubens, Reubens	40.00
Grangeville Savings & Trust Co., Grangeville	46.00
Bank of Winchester, Winchester	40.00
Bank of Gifford, Gifford	35.00
First Bank of Culdesac, Culdesac	40.00
Moscow State Bank, Moscow	53.50
Union State Bank, Nezperce	57.50
Bank of Camas Prairie, Grangeville	75.00
First State Bank, Kellogg	53.50
First Savings & Trust Co., Moscow	80.00
American Trust Company, Coeur d'Alene	67.50
Wallace Bank & Trust Company, Wallace	102.50
Weber Bank, Wardner	38.50
The State Bank, Idaho Falls	80.00
Coeur d'Alene Bank & Trust Co., Coeur d'Alene	57.50
Anderson Bros. Bank, Idaho Falls	105.00
Valley State Bank, Post Falls	40.00
D. W. Standrod & Co., Blackfoot	97.50

Bank of Montpelier, Montpelier	60.00
First Bank of Genesee, Genesee	47.50
Salmon River State Bank, Whitebird	57.50
Bear Lake State Bank, Paris	51.00
First State Bank, Teton City	38.50
Farmers State Bank, Tetonia	32.00
Cottonwood State Bank, Cottonwood	46.00
Bank of Ferdinand, Ferdinand	35.00
Victor State Bank, Victor	43.50
First State Bank, Drummond	32.00
Lava Hot Springs State Bank,	43.50
McCammon State Bank, McCammon	40.00
Downey State Bank, Downey	43.50
Farmers & Merchants Bank, Idaho Falls	87.50
Idaho State & Savings Bank, Preston	60.00
J. N. Ireland & Co., Malad	60.00
Bank of Aberdeen, Aberdeen	46.00
Anderson Bros. Bank, Rigby	20.00
Intermountain State Bank, Cascade	35.00
Bank of Orofino, Orofino	51.00
Potlatch State Bank, Potlatch	62.50
Ferdinand State Bank, Ferdinand	40.00
Fidelity State Bank, Orofino	47.50
State Bank of Peck, Peck	35.00
First Bank of Troy, Troy	61.00
Bank of Juliaetta, Juliaetta	35.00
First State Bank, Bovill	42.50
Latah County State Bank, Deary	40.00
Elk River State Bank, Elk River	40.00
First State Bank, St. Joe	28.50
Lumbermens State Bank, St. Maries	60.00
State Bank of Plummer, Plummer	40.00
State Bank of Worley, Worley	35.00
First Bank of Harrison, Harrison	42.50
Rathdrum State Bank, Rathdrum	46.00
Bank of Spirit Lake, Spirit Lake	46.00
Citizens State Bank, Priest River	40.00
First State Bank, Bonners Ferry	51.00
Bliss State Bank, Bliss	28.50
Heyburn State Bank, Heyburn	40.00
Stockgrowers Bank & Trust Co., Pocatello	92.50
First State Bank, Challis	46.00
Union Central Bank, May	38.50
Security State Bank, Ashton	72.50
St. Anthony Bank & Trust Co., St. Anthony	60.00
Farmers & Merchants Bank, Rexburg	60.00
Jefferson State Bank, Menan	43.50
Pioneer Bank & Trust Co., Salmon	57.50
Lemhi Valley Bank, Leadore	43.50
Farmers & Stockgrowers Bank, Montour	43.50
Farmers State Bank, New Plymouth	46.00
Fruitland State Bank, Fruitland	51.00
Genesee Exchange Bank, Genesee	53.50
Bank of Washington County, Midvale	52.50
Weiser Loan & Trust Co., Weiser	72.50
Bank of Emmett, Emmett	72.50
Glenns Ferry Bank, Glenns Ferry	51.00
Anderson Bros. Bank, Rigby (penalty)	50.00
Bank of Hollister, Hollister	43.50
Bank of Kimberly, Kimberly	51.00
Burley State Bank, Burley	80.00
Farmers & Merchants Bank, Rupert	43.50
Bank of Hansen, Hansen	51.00

Bank of Castleford, Castleford	32.00
Bank of Murtaugh, Murtaugh	38.50
Farmers & Merchants Bank, Filer	46.00
Bank of Rogerson, Rogerson	46.00
Paul State Bank, Paul	40.00
D. L. Evans & Co., Albion	43.50
Farmers Commercial & Savings Bank, Oakley	46.00
Oakley State Bank, Oakley	46.00
Citizens State Bank, Buhl	80.00
Idaho State Bank, Twin Falls	60.00
Twin Falls Bank & Trust Co., Twin Falls	92.50
Bank of Commerce, Burley	74.50
Hazelton State Bank, Hazelton	46.00
Eden State Bank, Eden	46.00
American Trust Co., Coeur d'Alene	67.50
Coeur d'Alene Bank & Trust Co.	57.50
Valley State Bank, Post Falls	40.00
Citizens State Bank, Priest River	42.50
Bank of Spirit Lake, Spirit Lake	46.00
Rathdrum State Bank, Rathdrum	46.00
First State Bank, Bonners Ferry	51.00
Bank of Orofino, Orofino	53.50
First State Bank, St. Joe	35.00
Elk River State Bank, Elk River	40.00
First State Bank, Bovill	42.50
Latah County State Bank, Deary	40.00
State Bank of Plummer, Plummer	40.00
State Bank of Worley, Worley	35.00
Potlatch State Bank, Potlatch	62.50
Bank of Stites, Stites	28.50
State Bank of Kooskia, Kooskia	42.50
State Bank of Kamiah, Kamiah	51.00
Fidelity State Bank, Orofino	42.50
State Bank of Peck, Peck	35.00
First Bank of Troy, Troy	51.00
Kendrick State Bank, Kendrick	42.50
The Farmers Bank, Kendrick	40.00
Bank of Juliaetta, Juliaetta	35.00
Lumbermens State Bank, St. Maries	60.00
First Bank of Harrison, Harrison	42.50
Weber Bank, Wardner	38.50
First State Bank, Kellogg	57.50
Wallace Bank & Trust Co., Wallace	102.50
Ft. Lapwai State Bank, Lapwai	38.50
Farmers Bank, Star	46.00
State Bank of Middleton, Middleton	40.00
Bank of Eagle, Eagle	46.00
Meridian State Bank, Meridian	43.50
First State Bank, Donnelly	35.00
First State Bank, Horseshoe Bend	28.50
Intermountain State Bank, Cascade	17.41
Farmers & Stockgrowers Bank, Montour	43.50
Bliss State Bank, Bliss	35.00
Carey State Bank, Carey	50.00
First State Bank, Richfield	43.50
Picabo State Bank, Picabo	43.50
Evans State Bank, American Falls	51.00
First Savings Bank, Pocatello	57.50
First State Bank, Rockland	35.00
McCammon State Bank, McCammon	40.00
Lava Hot Springs State Bank	38.50
The Commercial Bank, Shelley	51.00
D. W. Standrod & Co., Blackfoot	92.50

Lemhi Valley Bank, Leadore 43.50
Pioneer Bank & Trust Co., Salmon 57.50
Union Central Bank, May 38.50
First State Bank, Challis 46.00
W. G. Jenkins & Co., Mackay 57.50
Butte County Bank, Arco 38.50
Security State Bank, Ashton 67.50
First State Bank, Drummond 32.00
Victor State Bank, Victor 43.50
Fremont County Bank, Sugar City 51.00
First State Bank, Teton City 38.50
Salmon River State Bank, Whitebird (penalty) 50.00
Farmers State Bank, Tetonia 38.50
Bellevue Bank & Trust Co., Bellevue (Charter) .. 35.00
Federal State Bank, Preston (Charter) 30.00
Anderson Bros. Bank, Idaho Falls 105.00
Coeur d'Alene Bank & Trust Co., refund of ex-
    penses incurred during closing process 342.38
Bank of Roberts, Roberts 38.50
Anderson Bros. Bank, Rigby 43.50
Rexburg State Bank, Rexburg 70.00
Blackfoot City Bank, Blackfoot 60.00
Citizens Bank, Pocatello 92.50
Bank of Aberdeen, Aberdeen 46.00
St. Anthony Bank & Trust Co., St. Anthony 60.00
Bank of Soda Springs, Soda Springs 43.50
Farmers & Merchants Bank, Idaho Falls 82.50
Citizens State Bank, Gooding 51.00
The State Bank, Idaho Falls 80.00

Total for 1920 ....$12,188.29

BANKS CHARTERED

First Bank of Homedale, Homedale, Idaho, No. 173, opened February 7,
    1920, Capital $25,000.00.
Bank of Castleford, Castleford, Idaho, No. 174, opened March 29, 1920, Cap-
    ital $25,000.00.
Culdesac State Bank, Culdesac, Idaho, No. 175; opened June 8, 1920, Capi-
    tal $25,000.00.
Clearwater Valley State Bank, Kamiah, Idaho, No. 176, opened November 8,
    1920, Capital $25,000.00.
Federal State Bank, Preston, No. 177; opened December 20, 1920, Capital
    $25,000.00.

BANKS INCREASING CAPITAL STOCK.

Eden State Bank, Eden, $15,000 to $25,000, August 3, 1920.
Largilliere Company, Soda Springs, $10,000 to $25,000, January 1, 1920.
Boise Basin Bank, Idaho City, $12,950 to $15,000, May 28, 1920.
Citizens Bank, Pocatello, $100,000 to $300,000, June 30, 1920.
Bank of Roberts, Roberts, $10,000 to $25,000, June 30, 1920.
Lumbermens State Bank, St. Maries, $25,000 to $50,000, July 1, 1920.
Kuna State Bank, Kuna, $15,000 to $25,000, March 1, 1920.
Burley State Bank, Burley, $50,000 to $89,400, March 10, 1920.
Ilo State Bank, Craigmont, $10,000 to $25,000, April 12, 1920.
Fruitland State Bank, Fruitland, $10,000 to $25,000, March 27, 1920.
Idaho State & Savings Bank, Preston, $25,000 to $50,000, June 4, 1920.
Farmers State Bank, Tetonia, $15,000 to $25,000, May 12, 1920.
First State Bank, Richfield, $20,000 to $25,000, August 21, 1920.

STATE BANKS NATIONALIZED.

Bank of Commerce, Arco, to First National Bank, Arco, July 23, 1920.

STATE BANKS CHANGING NAME AND LOCATION.

Boise Basin Bank, Idaho City, to First State Bank, Horseshoe Bend, May 28, 1920.

STATE BANKS CHANGING LOCATION

Farmers & Stockgrowers Bank, Sweet to Montour.

STATE BANKS CONSOLIDATED

Stockgrowers Bank & Trust Company, Pocatelo, consolidated with National Bank of Idaho, Pocatello, October 13, 1920.

BANKS LIQUIDATED BY THE DEPARTMENT

Commercial & Savings Bank, Mountainhome, September 27, 1920.
Grangeville Savings & Trust Bank, Grangeville, November 29, 1920.
Coeur d'Alene Bank & Trust Co., Coeur d'Alene, November 3, 1920.

STATE BANK MEMBERS OF FEDERAL RESERVE SYSTEM.

		Date Admitted
Arco	Butte County Bank	Dec. 10, 1919
Ashton	Security State Bank	August 6, 1918
Bellevue	Bellevue State Bank	May 12, 1919
Blackfoot	Blackfoot City Bank	May 22, 1918
Blackfoot	D. W. Standrod & Co.	Feb. 2, 1920
Burley	Burley State Bank	Jan. 27, 1920
Cambridge	Peoples Bank	Sept. 26, 1918
Castleford	Bank of Castleford	April 30, 1920
Drummond	First State Bank	June 9, 1919
Eagle	Bank of Eagle	April 14, 1919
Emmett	Bank of Emmett	August 9, 1918
Filer	Farmers & Merchants Bank	Feb. 16, 1918
Genesee	Genesee Exchange Bank	Oct. 13, 1917
Gooding	Citizens State Bank	June 12, 1918
Grangeville	Bank of Camas Prairie	April 14, 1919
Hansen	Bank of Hansen	Feb. 28, 1920
Homedale	First Bank of Homedale	Feb. 20, 1920
Idaho Falls	Anderson Bros. Bank	Aug. 1, 1918
Idaho Falls	Farmers & Merchants Bank	August 12, 1918
Kimberly	Bank of Kimberly	Dec. 3, 1917
Kuna	Kuna State Bank	June 4, 1920
Malad	J. N. Ireland & Co.	Nov. 24, 1920

May	Union Central Bank	Oct. 24, 1918
Menan	Jefferson State Bank	Dec. 9, 1918
Meridian	Meridian State Bank	June 26, 1918
Montour	Farmers & Stockgrowers Bank	Sept. 5, 1918
Murtaugh	Bank of Murtaugh	August 5, 1918
Nezperce	Union State Bank	Oct. 29, 1918
Oakley	Farmers Com'l & Savings Bank	March 11, 1919
Orofino	Bank of Orofino	Oct. 14, 1918
Picabo	Picabo State Bank	Oct. 21, 1918
Pocatello	Citizens Bank	Jan. 2, 1919
Potlatch	Potlatch State Bank	Oct. 2, 1918
Rexburg	Farmers & Merchants Bank	April 9, 1918
Rupert	Farmers & Merchants Bank	Feb. 18, 1920
St. Anthony	St. Anthony Bank & Trust Co.	May 16, 1918
Star	Farmers Bank	Dec. 19, 1918
Sugar City	Fremont County Bank	April 9, 1918
Teton City	First State Bank	Nov. 4, 1919
Tetonia	Farmers State Bank	July 31, 1920
Twin Falls	Twin Falls Bank & Trust Co.	Jan. 21, 1919
Victor	Victor State Bank	August 12, 1918

ABERDEEN

BANK OF ABERDEEN

E. M. Brass .... President
M. A. Fugate .... Vice-President
P. A. Fugate .... Cashier
H. C. Wiebe .... Asst. Cashier
  Directors—E. M. Brass, M. A. Fugate, P. A. Fugate, H. C. Wiebe, G. W. Fugate.

Statement November 15, 1920

RESOURCES

Cash on hand ....$	4,794.54
Due from Banks	32,170.36
Checks and drafts on other banks	142.25
Other cash items	651.57
Loans and Discounts	203,446.82
Overdrafts	None
Stocks, Bonds and Warrants	18,968.52
Banking House, Furniture and Fixtures	5,620.93
Expenses in excess of earnings	2,189.88
Total ....$	$267,984.87

LIABILITIES

Individaul deposits subject to check ....$	$115,953.32
Time certificates of deposit	25,986.78
Cashier's checks	1,959.07
Certified checks	85.29
Due to other Banks (Deposits	4,000.41
Total Deposits	147,984.87
Capital Stock paid in	20,000.00
Surplus	10,000.00
Bills Payable, including obligations representing money borrowed	90,000.00
Re-Discounts	None
Other liabilities	None
Total ....$	$267,984.87

ALBION

D. L. EVANS & CO., BANKERS

Norman Isaachson .... President
L. L. Evans .... Vice-President
Robert Lounsbury .... Cashier
  Directors—Norman Isaachson, L. L. Evans, Robt. Lounsbury, D. W. Standrod, Wm. Jones.

Statement November 15, 1920

RESOURCES

Cash on hand ....$	3,957.24
Due from banks	9,953.60
Checks and drafts on other banks	135.83
Other cash items	1,420.59
Loans and discounts	131,104.17
Stocks, bonds & warrants	7,400.00
Banking House, furniture and fixtures	14,750.00
Total ....$	$168,721.43

LIABILITIES

Individual deposits subject to check ....$	$ 66,066.60
Savings deposits	296.29
Time certificates	30,707.46
Cashier's checks	50.00
Total deposits	97,120.35
Capital stock paid in	25,000.00
Surplus	8,000.00
Undivided profits, less interest, expenses and taxes paid	3,601.08
Bills payable, including obligation representing borrowed money	35,000.00
Total ....$	$168,721.43

AMERICAN FALLS

EVANS STATE BANK

L. L. Evans .... President
H. P. Houtz .... Vice-President
H. C. Allen .... Cashier
C. Lee French .... Asst. Cashier
A. C. Sallee .... Asst. Cashier
Directors—L. L. Evans, H. P. Houtz
H. C. Allen, D. W. Standrod, L. L.
Evans, Jr.

Statement November 15, 1920

RESOURCES

Cash on hand ....$	5,177.95
Due from banks	15,583.87
Checks and drafts on other banks	2,225.86
Other cash items	4,332.61
Loans and discounts	326,304.69
Overdrafts ....None	
Stocks, bonds & warrants	19,518.50
Premium on bonds ....None	
Claims, judgments, etc. ....None	
Furniture and fixtures	3,800.00
Other real estate	13,222.52
Other resources, collections in transit	1,475.85
Total ....$	391,641.85

LIABILITIES

Individual deposits subject to check ....$	191,450.62
Savings deposits	10,582.85
Postal Savings deposits .... None	
Demand certificates of deposit	25.00
Time certificates of deposit	46,056.60
Cashier's checks	4,590.89
Certified checks .... None	
Due to other banks (deposits)	62,554.49
Dividends unpaid .... None	
Total Deposits ....$	315,260.45
Capital stock paid in	25,000.00
Surplus	5,000.00
Undivided profits, less expenses, interest and taxes paid	6,381.40
Reserved for taxes .... None	
Bills payable, including obligations representing money borrowed	35,000.00
Re-Discounts	5,000.00
Other liabilities .... None	
Total ....$	391,641.85

ARCO

BUTTE COUNTY BANK

E. P. Armstrong ....President
Oscar C. Paisley ....Vice President
Otto H. Hoebel ....Cashier
G. M. McCandless............Asst. Cashier
Directors—R. W. Ferris, O. P. Williams, Thos. D. Perry, R. B. Merrill,
E. P. Armstrong, Oscar C. Paisley,
Otto H. Hoebel.

Statement November 15th, 1920.

RESOURCES

Cash on hand ....$	3,064.28
Due from Banks	25,656.62
Checks and Drafts on other Banks	1,985.67
Loans and Discounts	66,119.18
Overdrafts	249.06
Stocks, Bonds and Warrants	12,398.16
Banking House, Furniture and Fixtures	12,152.92
Other Resources, Interest earned, uncollected	1,151.01
Total ....$	122,776.90

LIABILITIES

Individual deposits subject to check ....$	73,038.21
Savings deposits	2,217.68
Time certs. of deposit	6,551.00
Cashier's checks	139.40
Total deposits	81,946.29
Capital stock paid in	25,000.00
Undivided profits, less expenses, interest and taxes paid	414.32
Re-discounts	15,308.00
Other liabilities. Reserved for bond depreciation	95.80
Reserved for interest	12.49
Total ....$	122,776.90

ASHTON

SECURITY STATE BANK

W. L. Robinson ....President
R. I. Rankin ....Vice-Pres.
Fred Swanstrum ....Vice-Pres.
Stanley G. Robinson .... Cashier
Stella Winfrey .... Asst. Cashier
Directors—W. L. Robinson, R. I.
Rankin, Fred Swanstrum, Stanley G.
Robinson, J. Harshbarger, Hubert
Thomas, Mal Anderson, J. E. Win-
frey, Henry Peterson.

Statement November 15, 1920

RESOURCES.

Cash on hand ....$	2,836.69
Due from banks	18,193.81
Checks and drafts on other	
Banks	3,122.03
Other cash items	1,300.60
Loans and discounts	554,831.60
Stocks, bonds and warrants	93,742.85
Banking house, furniture	
and fixtures	13,372.65
Other real estate	7,397.11
Stock in federal reserve	
bank	2,250.00
Expenses in excess of	
earnings	4,548.36
Total $701,595.70	

LIABILITIES

Individual deposits subject	
to check $173,367.62	
Time certs. of deposit	105,634.61
Cashier's checks	5,894.58
Total deposits $284,896.81	
Capital stock paid in	50,000.00
Surplus	25,000.00
Bills payable, including ob-	
ligations representing	
money borrowed	85,000.00
Re-discounts	256,698.89
Total $701,595.70	

BELLEVUE

BELLEVUE STATE BANK

Thos. D. Perry .... President
E. P. Armstrong .... Vice-Pres.
R. B. Merrill .... Cashier
Directors—Thos. D. Perry, E. P.
Armstrong, R. B. Merrill, Francis
Jones, Nick Werry.

Statement November 15, 1920

RESOURCES

Cash on hand ....$	3,376.35
Due from banks	17,779.63
Other cash items	100.00
Loans and discounts	266,317.50
Overdrafts	3,978.35
Stocks, bonds & warrants	9,842.11
Claims, judgments, etc.	740.95
Banking house, furniture	
and fixtures	8,875.00
Other real estate	19,418.83
Other resources	1,542.86
Total $331,971.58	

LIABILITIES

Individual deposits subject	
to check $117,655.94	
Savings deposits	34,022.86
Demand certs. of deposit ..	2,295.06
Time certs. of deposit	21,371.30
Cashier's checks	8,547.65
Due to other banks (de-	
posits)	303.65
Dividends unpaid	74.00
Total deposits $184,260.46	
Capital stock paid in	30,000.00
Surplus	16,443.71
Undivided profits, less ex-	
penses, interest and tax-	
es paid	1,721.11
Bills Payable, including ob-	
ligations representing	
money borrowed	35,000.00
Re-discounts	64,535.93
Other liabilities	.37
Total $331,971.58	

BLACKFOOT

BLACKFOOT CITY BANK

Nofear Davis .... President
P. G. Johnston .... Vice-Pres.
Louis Felt .... Vice-Pres.
F. J. Stone .... Cashier
Directors—Nofear Davis, P. G. Johnston, Louis Felt, F. J. Stone, J. O. Morgan, Michael Barclay, B. F. Blodgett, Jas. Duckworth.

Statement November 15, 1920

RESOURCES

Cash on hand ....$	8,195.92
Due from banks	217,428.59
Checks and drafts on other banks	27,177.81
Other cash items	602.22
Loans and discounts	285,850.95
Overdrafts	None
Stocks, bonds & warrants..	165,556.70
Banking house, furniture and fixtures	11,951.40
Other real estate	11,655.90
Other resources	8,015.42
Total ....$	646,434.91

LIABILITIES

Individual deposits subject to check ....$	311,625.22
Savings deposits	34,643.09
Time certs. of deposit	3,154.54
Cashier's checks	17,968.90
Total deposits	367,391.75
Capital stock paid in	50,000.00
Surplus	10,000.00
Undivided profits, less expenses, interest and taxes paid	3,589.97
Bills payable, including obligations representing borrowed money	176,000.00
Rediscounts	37,801.93
Other liabilities	151.26
Total ....$	646,434.91

BLACKFOOT

D. W. STANDROD & COMPANY, BANKERS.

C. W. Berryman .... President
Geo. F. Gagon .... Vice-Pres.
W. F. Berryman .... Cashier
W. D. Gagon .... Asst. Cashier
E. E. Sanders .... Asst. Cashier
Directors—C. W. Berryman, Geo. F. Gagon, L. L. Evans, D. W. Standrod, D. L. Evans.

Statement November 15, 1920

RESOURCES

Cash on hand ....$	22,117.34
Due from banks	143,811.38
Checks and drafts on other banks	87,657.56
Other cash items	3,529.51
Loans and discounts	1,896,835.00
Overdrafts	None
Stocks, bonds & warrants..	696,510.36
Premium on bonds	None
Federal Reserve stock	5,550.00
Banking house, furniture and fixtures	38,661.70
Other real estate	6,004.62
Other resources, due us on Liberty Bonds	116.34
Total ....$	2,900,793.81

LIABILITIES

Individual deposits subject to check ....$	704,454.90
Savings deposits	141,989.32
Postal savings deposits	81.13
Demand certs. of deposit ..	177.00
Time certs. of deposit	114,339.19
Cashier's checks	34,207.50
Certified checks	53.76
Due to other banks (deposits)	288,153.47
Dividends unpaid	6,000.00
Total deposits	1,289,456.27
Capital stock paid in	100,000.00
Surplus	85,000.00
Undivided profits, less expenses, interest and taxes paid	4,409.10
Reserved for taxes	None
Bills payable, including obligations representing money borrowed	516,700.00
Re-discounts	787,728.44
Other liabilities, bonds borrowed	117,500.00
Total ....$	2,900,793.81

BLISS

BLISS STATE BANK.

Geo. W. Hulme .... President
R. B. Thorpe .... Vice-Pres.
S. W. Strubble .... Cashier

Directors—Geo. W. Hulme, R. B.
Thorpe, S. W. Strubble, M. E. Bilhoit,
Frank Tarpning.

Statement November 15, 1920

RESOURCES

Cash on hand ....$	2,542.10
Due from banks	4,852.56
Checks and drafts on other banks	52.67
Other cash items	3.43
Loans and discounts	87,303.55
Overdrafts	162.95
Stocks, bonds & warrants..	6,615.19
Banking house, furniture and fixtures	1,700.00
Other resources	787.07
Expenses in excess of earnings	1,202.63
Total ....$	105,222.15

LIABILITIES

Individual deposits subject to check ....$	41,849.98
Time certs. of deposit	7,157.93
Cashier's checks	1,214.24
Total deposits	50,222.15
Capital stock paid in	10,000.00
Surplus	3,000.00
Bills payable, including obligations representing money borrowed	42,000.00
Total ....$	105,222.15

BOISE

BOISE TITLE & TRUST COMPANY

S. H. Hays .... President
O. O. Haga .... Vice-Pres.
W. J. Abbs .... Secretary
R. S. Hoover .... Treasurer

Directors—E. M. Hoover, L. H. Cox
C. L. Joy, S. H. Hays, O. O. Haga,
W. J. Abbs, R. S. Hoover.

Statement November 15, 1920

RESOURCES

Cash on hand ....$	2,817.81
Due from banks	7,962.68
Checks and drafts on other banks	171.10
Other cash items	244.35
Loans and discounts	60,551.27
Stocks, bonds & warrants..	28,280.25
Abstract plant, insurance plant, safe deposit vault, furniture and fixtures	51,645.55
Other real estate	72,213.95
Other resources, accounts receivable	4,398.01
Savings investments	42,149.47
Trust investments	13,500.00
Total ....$	283,934.44

LIABILITIES

Savings deposits ....$	69,891.70
Demand certs. of deposit ..	1,955.00
Time certs. of deposit	13,527.55
Trust deposits	61,932.64
Total deposits	147,306.89
Capital stock paid in	100,000.00
Surplus	14,000.00
Undivided profits, less expenses, interest and taxes paid	7,627.55
Bills payable, including obligations representing money borrowed	15,000.00
Total ....$	283,934.44

BONNERS FERRY

FIRST STATE BANK

F. W. Anderson .... President
Chas. O'Callaghan .... Vice-Pres.
J. B. Cowen .... Cashier
J. A. Hanson .... Asst. Cashier
M. F. Muhlfeld .... Asst. Cashier

Directors—F. W. Anderson, Charles O'Callaghan, J. B. Cowen, Mike Fitzpatrick, F. R. Anderson.

Statement November 15, 1920

RESOURCES

Cash on hand	$ 23,017.50
Due from banks	31,789.68
Checks and drafts on other banks	1,990.87
Loans and discounts	302,378.48
Overdrafts	790.67
Stocks, bonds & warrants..	46,436.54
Banking house, furniture and fixtures	14,975.00
Other real estate	5,645.06
Total	$427,032.80

LIABILITIES

Individual deposits subject to check	229,868.44
Savings deposits	78,497.04
Postal savings deposits	874.41
Time certs. of deposit	66,175.25
Cashier's checks	3,923.15
Certified checks	2,342.20
Total deposits	381,680.49
Capital stock paid in	30,000.00
Surplus	3,000.00
Undivided profits, less expenses, interest and taxes paid	8,352.31
Re-discounts	4,000.00
Total	$427,032.80

BOVILL

FIRST STATE BANK

J. A. Harsh .... President
T. P. Jones .... Vice-Pres.
S. H. Crotinger .... Cashier
H. MacGowan .... Asst. Cashier

Directors—J. A. Harsh, T. P. Jones S. H. Crotinger, G. E. Harsh, L. M. Harsh.

Statement November 15, 1920

RESOURCES

Cash on hand	$ 10,281.85
Due from banks	89,740.05
Other cash items	273.78
Loans and discounts	122,819.48
Overdrafts	10.96
Stocks, bonds & warrants..	75,255.81
Banking house, furniture and fixtures	8,600.00
Total	$306,981.93

LIABILITIES

Individual deposits subject to check	116,863.56
Postal savings deposits	3,914.10
Demand certs. of deposit ..	150,240.02
Cashier's checks	16,175.75
Certified checks	4.30
Total deposits	287,197.73
Capital stock paid in	10,000.00
Surplus	5,000.00
Undivided profits, less expenses, interest and taxes paid	4,784.20
Total	$306,981.93

BRUNEAU

BRUNEAU STATE BANK

Arthur Pence ....President
J. F. Noble ....Vice President
M. E. Reynolds ....Cashier

Directors—Arthur Pence, J. F. Noble, M. E. Reynolds, S. P. Noble, Arthur Pence, Jr.

Statement November 15, 1920

RESOURCES

Cash on hand (lawful money of the U. S.) ....$	4,989.37
Due from Banks	6,584.54
Other cash items	349.64
Loans and discounts	214,389.42
Stocks, Bonds and Warrants	9,534.44
Banking house, Furniture and Fixtures	5,500.00
Other Resources	305.85
Total ....$	241,623.27

LIABILITIES

Individual deposits subject to check ....$	103,924.29
Time certs. of deposit	70,769.17
Cashier's checks	241.43
Due to other banks (deposits)	8,802.32
Total deposits ....$	183,937.24
Capital stock paid in	25,000.00
Surplus fund	12,500.00
Undivided profits, less expense, interest and taxes paid	5,836.06
Bills payable, including obligations representing money borrowed	14,350.00
Total ....$	241,623.27

BUHL

CITIZENS STATE BANK

J. W. Hayward ....President
C. C. Griffin ....Vice President
Russ W. Allred ....Cashier
Glenn F. Fritcher ....Asst. Cashier

Directors—J. J. Rugg, J. W. Hayward, C. C. Griffin, Russ W. Allred, Glenn F. Fritcher.

Statement November 15, 1920

RESOURCES

Cash on hand ....$	12,734.41
Due from banks	51,741.64
Checks and drafts on other banks	6,202.37
Other cash items	2,757.72
Loans and discounts	991,793.25
Overdrafts	6,403.28
Stocks, bonds, warrants..	26,674.71
Banking house, furniture and fixtures	41,818.36
Other real estate	6,960.00
Total ....$	1,147,085.74

LIABILITIES

Individual deposits subject to check ....$	492,369.88
Time certificates of deposit	96,558.43
Cashiers's checks	53,190.48
Due to other banks (deposits)	5,452.81
Total deposits	647,571.60
Capital stock paid in	100,000.00
Surplus	25,000.00
Undivided profits, less expenses, interest and taxes paid	6,429.52
Bills payable, including obligations representing money borrowed	237,500.00
Re-discounts	130,584.62
Total ....$	1,147,085.74

BURLEY

BANK OF COMMERCE

C. M. Oberholtzer ....President
J. P. Davis .... Vice President
D. L. Wyland ....Vice President
W. C. Dickey ....Cashier
Directors—C. M. Oberholtzer, J. P. Davis, D. L. Wyland, G. O. Paulson, H. J. Nichols.

Statement November 15, 1920

RESOURCES

Cash on hand ....$	15,429.96
Due from banks	40,333.53
Checks and drafts on other banks	8,627.63
Loans and discounts	937,970.40
Stocks, bonds & warrants	15,196.91
U. S. Bonds and War Savings Stamps	84,568.11
Banking house, furniture and fixtures	9,436.14
Other real estate	1,957.20
Total ....$	**1,113,519.88**

LIABILITIES

Individual deposits subject to check	349,288.73
Savings deposits	16,583.32
Demand certs. of deposit ..	7,445.15
Time certs of deposit	258,517.78
Cashier's checks	29,985.16
Certified checks	312.48
Due to other banks (deposits)	765.85
Dividends unpaid	175.00
Total deposits	663,074.47
Capital stock paid in	50,000.00
Surplus	15,000.00
Undivided profits, less expense, interest and taxes paid	20,237.16
Bills payable secured by U. S. Bonds	60,000.00
Bills payable including obligations representing money borrowed	154,500.00
Rediscounts	140,708.25
Bonds borrowed	10,000.00
Total ....$	**1,113,519.88**

BURLEY

BURLEY STATE BANK

S. Grover Rich .... President
W. L. Burton .... Vice-Pres.
W. A. Budge .... Vice-Pres.
Will H. Young .... Cashier
Directors—E. J. Larson, R. C. Rich, J. W. Hoppe, S. Grover Rich, W. L. Burton W. A. Budge, Will H. Young.

Statement November 15, 1920

RESOURCES

Cash on hand ....$	13,400.43
Due from banks	37,934.58
Checks and drafts on other banks	10,458.79
Other cash items	35,465.29
Loans and discounts	1,215,812.85
Stocks, bonds & warrants	54,689.80
Banking house, furniture and fixtures	18,600.00
Other real estate	7,598.34
Other resources	3,915.19
Federal Reserve bank stk	1,800.00
Total ....$	**1,399,675.27**

LIABILITIES

Individual deposits subject to check	318,305.03
Savings deposits	7,885.81
Time certs. of deposit	184,624.74
Cashier's checks	10,911.86
Certified checks	199.77
Due to other banks (deposits)	60,013.52
Dividends unpaid	1,010.00
Total deposits	582,950.73
Capital stock paid in	89,400.00
Surplus	17,880.00
Undivided profits, less expenses, interest and taxes paid	13,711.43
Bills payable, including obligations representing money borrowed	245,600.00
Re-discounts	441,433.11
Other liabilities, acceptors liability	8,700.00
Total ....$	**1,399,675.27**

CALDWELL

CALDWELL COMMERCIAL BANK

John C. Rice .... President
J. H. Lowell .... Vice-President
E. H. Plowhead .... Cashier
C. L. Sloan .... Asst. Cashier

Directors—Robt. Aikman, A. Greenlund, A. A. Binford, J. W. Thompson, A. Ballantyne, F. O. Chaney, John C. Rice, J. H. Lowell, E. H. Plowhead.

Statement November 15, 1920

RESOURCES

Cash on hand	$ 16,397.59
Due from banks	85,300.98
Checks and drafts on other banks	12,034.99
Other cash items	5,456.00
Loans and discounts	825,698.12
Stocks, bonds & warrants	107,846.73
Banking house, furniture and fixtures	55,000.00
Other real estate	4,560.00
Total	**$1,112,294.41**

LIABILITIES

Individual deposits subject to check	466,054.71
Savings deposits	136.948.89
Demand certs. of deposit	7,171.13
Time certs. of deposit	140,095.79
Due to other banks (deposits)	13,161.15
Total deposits	**763,431.67**
Capital stock paid in	100.000.00
Surplus	40,000.00
Undivided profits, less expenses and taxes paid	5,821.74
Bills payable, including obligations representing money borrowed	201,000.00
Depreciative reserve	2,041.00
Total	**$1,112,294.41**

CAMBRIDGE

PEOPLES BANK

W. H. Eckles .... President
Fred W. Jewel .... Vice-President
A. W. Gipson .... Cashier

Directors—W. H. Eckles, Fred W. Jewell, A. W. Gipson, Harry M. Coon, H. W. Lyons.

Statement November 15, 1920

RESOURCES

Cash on hand	$ 4,914.97
Due from banks	37,783.78
Loans and discounts	268,196.37
Overdrafts	293.66
Stocks, bonds & warrants	14,400.00
Banking house, furniture and fixtures	7,000.00
Other real estate	957.00
Other resources, collections in transit	3,000.00
Total	**$336,545.78**

LIABILITIES

Individual deposits subject to check	184,529.58
Demand certs. of deposit	6,511.10
Time certs. of deposit	62,788.51
Total deposits	**253,829.19**
Capital stock paid in	40,000.00
Surplus	6,000.00
Undivided profits, less expenses, interest and taxes paid	10,016.59
Bills payable, including obligations representing money borrowed	11,800.00
Re-discounts	14,900.00
Total	**$336,545.78**

CAREY

CAREY STATE BANK

Irvin Payne .... President
Thos. C. Stanford .... Vice-President
C. M. Chidester .... Cashier

Directors—Ira Eldredge, W. F. Rawson, W. L. Adamson, S. Parker Richards, Irvin Payne, Thos. C. Stanford, Jos. S. Cooper.

Statement November 15, 1920

RESOURCES

Cash on hand ....$	5,077.70
Due from banks	27,557.87
Loans and discounts	172,677.24
Overdrafts	117.38
Stocks, bonds & warrants	4,112.63
Banking house, furniture and fixtures	4,200.00
Total ....$	213,742.82

LIABILITIES

Individual deposits subject to check	71,484.81
Savings deposits	905.60
Time certs. of deposit	24,951.15
Cashier's checks	11,591.67
Certified checks	150.00
Total deposits	109,083.23
Capital stock paid in	40,000.00
Surplus	10,000.00
Undivided profits	1,381.09
Bills payable	45,000.00
Re-discounts	5,000.00
Other liabilities	3,278.50
Total ....$	213,742.82

CASCADE

INTERMOUNTAIN STATE BANK

L. M. Gorton .... President
T. L. Worthington .... Vice-Pres.
Wm. Mickelson .... Cashier

Directors—L. M. Gorton, T. L. Worthington, Andred Nelson.

Statement November 15, 1920

RESOURCES

Cash on hand ....$	9,984.19
Due from banks	26,309.09
Other cash items	159.89
Loans and discounts	65,504.70
Overdrafts	18.50
Stocks, bonds & warrants	19,051.07
Banking house, furniture and fixtures	7,811.15
Other resources	540.19
Total ....$	129,378.78

LIABILITIES

Individual deposits subject to check	103,737.81
Time certs. of deposit	7,663.30
Certified checks	530.00
Total deposits	111,931.11
Capital stock paid in	10,000.00
Surplus	6,000.00
Undivided profits, less expenses, interest and taxes paid	1,083.97
Reserved for taxes	363.70
Total ....$	129,378.78

CASTLEFORD

BANK OF CASTLEFORD

J. S. Bussell .... President
John A. Noble .... Vice-Pres.
E .T. Provost .... Cashier

Directors—J. S. Bussell, John A. Noble, Claud Brown, G. F. Thomas.

Statement November 15, 1920

RESOURCES

Cash on hand ....$	1,495.03
Due from banks	5,065.34
Loans and discounts	46,639.41
Overdrafts	112.36
Banking house, furniture and fixtures	7,910.69
Federal Reserve bank stk	800.00
Total ....$	62,022.83

LIABILITIES

Individual deposits subject to check	34,794.08
Time certs. of deposit	1,512.00
Cashier's checks	1,127.40
Total deposits	34,433.48
Capital stock paid in	25,000.00
Surplus	1,250.00
Undivided profits, less expenses, interest and taxes paid	1,076.85
Re-discounts	262.50
Total ....$	62,022.83

CHALLIS

FIRST STATE BANK

S. L. Reese .... President
E. J. Mitchell .... Vice-Pres.
E. W. Hovey .... Vice-Pres.
N. C. Hovey .... Cashier

Directors—H. H. Hartman, John Ostrom, F. A. Reed, F. Nickerson, S. L. Reece, E. J. Mitchell.

Statement November 15, 1920

RESOURCES

Cash on hand ....$	10,531.81
Due from banks	63,380.39
Other cash items	281.37
Loans and discounts	161,649.44
Stocks, bonds, warrants	18,727.51
Banking house, furniture and fixtures	4,700.00
Revenue stamps	151.98
Other resources, transit account	598.79
Total ....$	260,021.29

LIABILITIES

Individual deposits subject to check ....$	170,511.12
Time certs. of deposit	35,218.85
Cashier's checks	2,978,91
Dividends unpaid	100.00
Total deposits ....$	208,808.88
Capital stock paid in	20,000.00
Surplus	10,000.00
Undivided profits, less expenses, interest and taxes paid	6,212.41
Bills payable, including obligations representing money borrowed	15,000.00
Total ....$	260,021.29

COEUR D'ALENE

AMERICAN TRUST COMPANY

Huntington Taylor .... President
A. V. Chamberlain .... Vice-Pres.
Ira H. Shallis .... Cashier
C. E. Allison .... Asst. Cashier
R. A. Hook .... Asst. Cashier

Directors—John J. O'Brien, T. J. Stonestreet, W. S. Rosenberry, Sig Hofslund, Huntington Taylor, A. V. Chamberlain, Ira H. Shallis.

Statement November 15, 1920.

RESOURCES

Cash on hand ....$	50,740.65
Due from banks	135,453.27
Checks and drafts on other banks	3,413.35
Other cash items	1,276.15
Loans and discounts	726,519.55
Overdrafts	4,869.59
Stocks, bonds & warrants	99,612.21
Prem. on bonds—none.	
Claims, judgments, etc.—none.	
Banking house, furniture and fixtures	11,762.34
Other real estate	7,173.28
Other resources	29,356.85
Expenses in excess of earnings—none.	
Total ....$	1,070,177.24

LIABILITIES

Individual deposits subject to check	479,250.01
Savings deposits	331,914.23
Postal Sav. Dep.—None.	
Demand certs. of deposit	1,139.47
Expense vouchers	49.86
Time certs. of deposit	154,628.05
Cashier's checks	8,556.43
Certified checks	16.80
Due to other banks	18,471.06
Sundry accounts	100.65
Div. unpaid—None.	
Total deposits	994,180.56
Capital stock paid in	50,000.00
Surplus	8,000.00
Undivided profits, less expenses, interest and taxes paid	17,996.86
Total ....$	1,070,177.24

COTTONWOOD

COTTONWOOD STATE BANK

E. M. Ehrhardt .... President
M. M. Belknap .... Vice-Pres.
H. C. Matthiesen .... Cashier
A. H. Thaelke .... Asst. Cashier

Directors—E. M. Ehrhardt, M. M. Belknap, H. C. Mattiesen, Herman H. Nuxall, Herman von Bargen, Barney J. Stubbers, Barney Luchtefeld, Francis G. Nuxall.

Statement November 15, 1920

RESOURCES

Cash on hand ....$	8,061.20
Due from banks	12,646.32
Checks and drafts on other banks	887.97
Other cash items	3,105.77
Loans and discounts	266,692.04
Overdrafts	35.32
Stocks, bonds, warrants	33,324.73
Banking house, furniture and fixtures	6,587.35
Total ....$	331,340.70

LIABILITIES

Individual deposits subject to check ....$	132,143.73
Time certs. of deposit	119,085.80
Cashier's checks	2,502.58
Total deposits	253,732.11
Capital stock paid in	25,000.00
Surplus	10,000.00
Undivided profits, less expenses, interest and taxes paid	3,021.99
Reserved for taxes	554.10
Re-discounts	39,032.50
Total ....$	331,340.70

COUNCIL

FIRST BANK OF COUNCIL

Fred Cool .... President
W. M. Brown .... Vice-President
E. S. Clapp .... Cashier
Bert H. Smith .... Asst. Cashier

Directors—Fred Cool, W. M. Brown
E. S. Clapp, M. D. Chaffee, D. J. Donnelly.

Statement November 15, 1920

RESOURCES

Cash on hand ....$	6,564.89
Due from banks	33,811.08
Loans and discounts	187,910.72
Stocks, bonds, warrants	25,111.95
Claims, judgments, etc.	650.00
Banking house, furniture and fixtures	11,238.84
Other real estate	500.00
Total ....$	$265,787.48

LIABILITIES

Individual deposits subject to check ....$	$174,678.74
Savings deposits	3,459.84
Demand certs. of deposit ..	9.00
Time certs. of deposit	41,193.06
Cashier's checks	1,106.06
Certified checks	9.50
Total deposits ....$	$220,456.20
Capital stock paid in	25,000.00
Surplus	5,000.00
Undivided profits, less expenses, interest and taxes paid	5,947.34
Reserved for taxes	383.94
Bills payable, including obligations representing money borrowed	9,000.00
Total ....$	$265,787.48

CRAIGMONT

ILO STATE BANK.

P. J. Miller .... President
R. A. Dammrose .... Vice-Pres.
J. J. Mockler .... Cashier
R. S. Mathews .... Asst. Cashier

Directors—P. J. Miller, R. A.
Dammrose, J. J. Mockler, J. L. Osborn, C. E. Dunaway.

Statement November 15, 1920

RESOURCES

Cash on hand ....$	5,938.50
Due from banks	26,965.13
Checks and drafts on other banks	541.13
Other cash items	196.85
Loans and discounts	263,903.37
Overdrafts	1,210.75
Stocks, bonds, warrants	25,913.36
Banking house, furniture and fixtures	2,866.11
Other real estate	12,877.52
Total ....$	$340,412.72

LIABILITIES

Individual deposits subject to check ....$	$177,844.95
Demand certs. of deposit ..	5,630.50
Time certs. of deposit	118,623.76
Certified checks	23.00
Total deposits ....$	$302,122.21
Capital stock paid in	25,000.00
Surplus	5,000.00
Undivided profits, less expenses, interest and taxes paid	7,790.51
Reserved for taxes	500.00
Total ....$	$340,412.72

CRAIGMONT

BANK OF VOLLMER

A. E. Clarke .... President
E. W. Eaves .... Vice-Pres.
Walter Zimmerman .... Cashier

Directors—B. V. Badine, N. S. Vollmer-Hopkins, A. E. Kroutinger, A. E. Clarke; E. W. Eaves.

Statement November 15, 1920

RESOURCES

Cash on hand ....$	5,723.86
Due from banks	3,012.31
Checks and drafts on other banks	2,912.29
Other cash items	1,190.35
Loans and discounts	293,674.32
Stocks, bonds, warrants ..	19,072.73
Banking house, furniture and fixtures	9,000.00
Other real estate	2,691.96
Other resources (items in transit)	996.00
Revenue stamps	60.00
Total 338,333.82	

LIABILITIES

Individual deposits subject to check	151,678.78
Demand certs. of deposit ..	410.56
Time certs. of deposit	151,698.83
Cashier's checks	62.50
Due to other banks (deposits)	11,000.00
Total deposits	314,850.67
Capital stock paid in	15,000.00
Surplus	3,000.00
Undivided profits, less expenses, interest and taxes paid	5,483.15
Total 338,333.82	

CULDESAC

CULDESAC STATE BANK

E. M. Ehrhardt .... President
Theo Mattson .... Vice-Pres.
G. S. Porter .... Cashier

Directors—E. M. Ehrhardt, Theo Mattson, C. J. Norbo, Albert Sogard, E. A. Wyman, B. C. Barbor, A. C. Chace.

Statement November 15, 1920

RESOURCES

Cash on hand ....$	3,517.53
Due from banks	3,362.60
Checks and drafts on other banks	488.37
Loans and discounts	60,307.87
Overdrafts	240.34
Stocks, bonds, warrants	1,375.34
Banking house, furniture and fixtures	13,772.86
Total ....$ 83,064.91	

LIABILITIES

Individual deposits subject to check	32,202.54
Savings deposits	1,267.28
Time certs. of deposit	8,725.45
Cashier's checks	1,844.82
Total deposits	44,040.09
Capital stock paid in	15,000.00
Surplus	3,000.00
Undivided profits, less expenses, interest and taxes paid	5,439.82
Bills payable, including obligations representing money borrowed	10,000.00
Re-discounts	5,585.00
Total ....$ 83,064.91	

CULDESAC

FIRST BANK OF CULDESAC.

C. D. Updegraff .... President
E. W. Eaves .... Vice-Pres.
E. F. Persons .... Cashier

Directors—C. D. Updegraff, E. W. Eaves, A. E. Clarke, N. S. Vollmer-Hopkins.

Statement November 15, 1920

RESOURCES

Cash on hand ....$	7,730.61
Due from banks	10,941.42
Checks and drafts on other banks	362.30
Other cash items	704.83
Loans and discounts	176,518.92
Stocks, bonds, warrants ..	3,310.37
Banking house, furniture and fixtures	3,900.00
Other resources, revenue stamps, U. S. Bonds	4,423.22
Total ....$	207,891.67

LIABILITIES

Individual deposits subject to check	70,967.16
Demand certs. of deposit ..	3,557.52
Time certs. of deposit	89,306.54
Total deposits	163,831.22
Capital stock paid in	10,000.00
Surplus	2,000.00
Undivided profits, less expenses, interest and taxes paid	1,929.45
Reserved for taxes	131.00
Bills payable, including obligations representing money borrowed	30,000.00
Total ....$	207,891.67

DEARY

LATAH COUNTY STATE BANK

J. A. Harsh ....President
G. E. Harsh ....Vice President
G. H. Wylie ....Cashier

Directors— J. A. Harsh, G. E. Harsh, Martha E. Harsh, H. A. Warren, G. H. Wylie.

Statement November 15, 1920.

RESOURCES

Cash on hand ....$	8,093.47
Due from banks	14,849.41
Checks and drafts on other banks	200.00
Other cash items	436.13
Loans and discounts	133,410.28
Overdrafts	101.84
Stocks, bonds, & warrants	51,270.05
Claims, judgments, etc.......	414.00
Banking house, furniture and fixtures	7,500.00
Total ....$	216,275.18

LIABILITIES

Individual deposits subject to check ....$	109,170.18
Demand certificates of deposit	23,782.52
Time certificates of deposit	53,124.55
Cashier's checks	5,244.50
Certified checks	200.00
Due to other banks (deposits)	2,731.70
Total deposits	194,253.45
Capital stock paid in	15,000.00
Surplus	5,000.00
Undivided profits, less expenses, interest and taxes paid	2,021.73
Total ....$	216,275.18

DECLO

DECLO STATE BANK

Sam Gillett ....President
L. E. Olson .... Vice President
J. C. Darrington ....Vice President
Frank Brocksmith .... Cashier

Directors—J. C. Osterhout, Andy Anderson, T. A. Williams, Sam Gillett, L. E. Olson, J. C. Darrington.

Statement November 15, 1920.

RESOURCES

Cash on hand ....$	1,978.50
Due from banks	1,132.95
Other cash items	380.40
Loans and discounts	206,328.80
Stocks, bonds, warrants....	3,214.34
Claims, judgments, etc.......	1,608.54
Banking house, furniture and fixtures	8,898.04
Other real estate	35,120.27
Other resources	738.83
Total ....$	259,400.76

LIABILITIES

Individual deposits subject to check ....$	54,738.66
Savings deposits	196.64
Time certificates of deposit	35,824.55
Cashier's checks	3,594.59
Due to other banks (deposits)	24,398.88
Dividends unpaid	40.00
Total deposits	118,793.32
Capital stock paid in	25,000.00
Surplus	2,500.00
Undivided profits, less expenses, interest and taxes paid	568.28
Bills payable, including obligations representing money borrowed	30,000.00
Rediscounts	82,539.16
Total ....$	259,400.76

DONNELLY

FIRST STATE BANK

C. A. West ....President
R. B. Halferty ....Vice President
H. E. Armstrong .... Cashier

Directors—H. M. Cook, B. F. Roberts, R. L. West, C. A. West, R. B. Halferty, H. E. Armstrong.

Statement November 15, 1920.

RESOURCES

Cash on hand ....$	3,006.43
Due from banks	17,061.90
Checks and drafts on other banks	230.15
Other cash items	None
Loans and discounts	83,355.61
Overdrafts	None
Stocks, bonds & warrants	13,994.23
Banking house furniture and fixtures	4,317.92
Other real estate	2,826.17
Total ....$	124,792.41

LIABILITIES

Individual deposits subject to check ....$	87,828.14
Time certificates of deposit	10,403.05
Cashier's Checks	2,854.41
Total deposits	101,085.60
Capital stock paid in	10,000.00
Surplus	2,500.00
Undivided profits	1,206.81
Bills payable, including obligations representing money borrowed	10,000.00
Total ....$	124,792.41

DOWNEY

DOWNEY STATE BANK

Geo. T. Hyde ....President
W. H. Coffin ....Vice President
J. F. Sievers .... Cashier
G. D. Layton ....Asst. Cashier

Directors—Geo. T. Hyde, W. H. Coffin, J. F. Sievers, G. A. Sievers, A. Rieger.

Statement November 15, 1920

RESOURCES

Cash on hand ....$	3,461.66
Due from banks	22,576.76
Other cash items	53.65
Loans and discounts	123,290.12
Stocks, bonds & warrants	54,846.36
Banking house, furniture and fixtures	3,600.00
Total ....$	$207,828.55

LIABILITIES

Individual deposits subject to check ....$	$113,791.81
Savings deposits	7,595.60
Time certificates of deposit	18,273.80
Cashier's checks	4,466.00
Total deposits	144,127.21
Capital stock paid in	25,000.00
Surplus	5,000.00
Undivided profits, less expenses, interest and taxes paid	2,977.35
Bills payable, including obligations representing money borrowed	29,650.00
Reserve fund, Liberty bonds	1,073.99
Total ....$	$207,828.55

DRUMMOND

FIRST STATE BANK

L. H. Neal ....President
S. L. Reece .... Vice President
V. E. Gailey ....Vice President
I. E. Simpson ....Cashier

Directors—L. H. Neal, S. L. Reece, V. E. Gailey, F. A. Bailey, R. H. Pemble, C. N. Dedman.

Statement November 15, 1920

RESOURCES

Cash on hand ....$	906.71
Due from banks	4,470.10
Loans and discounts	62,250.32
Stocks, bonds, warrants	8,977.40
Banking house, furniture and fixtures	4,900.00
Revenue stamps	9.86
Total ....$	81,514.39

LIABILITIES

Individual deposits subject to check ....$	26,174.93
Demand certificates of deposit	865.84
Time certificates of deposit	4,194.00
Cashier's checks	1,048.16
Total deposits	32,282.93
Capital stock paid in	25,000.00
Undivided profits, less expenses, interest and taxes paid	3,661.31
Bills payable, including obligations representing money borrowed	5,000.00
Re-discounts	15,570.15
Total ....$	81,514.39

EAGLE

BANK OF EAGLE

Wm. Goodall ....President
F. I. Newhouse .... Vice President
E. H. Fikkan .... Cashier

Directors—C. D. Newhouse, E. C. Towne, Wm. Goodall, F. I. Newhouse, E. H. Fikkan.

Statement November 15, 1920

RESOURCES

Cash on hand ....$	1,786.75
Due from banks	40,719.31
Checks and drafts on other banks	5,122.28
Loans and discounts	206,400.16
Overdrafts	144.47
Stocks, bonds & warrants	13,182.45
Banking house, furniture and fixtures	5,857.50
Other real estate	1,015.42
Stock in Federal Reserve bank	850.00
Total ....$	275,078.34

LIABILITIES

Individual deposits subject to check	$191,641.41
Demand certificates of deposit	3,106.17
Time certificates of deposit	47,187.78
Cashier's checks	2,218.36
Certified checks	50.00
Total deposits	244,203.72
Capital stock paid in	25,000.00
Surplus	2,100.00
Undivided profits, less expenses, interest and taxes paid	3,774.62
Total ....$	275,078.34

EDEN.

EDEN STATE BANK

Willis J. Young .... President
D. R. Pingree ....Vice President
Earl S. Young ....Cashier

Directors—Willis J. Young, D. R. Pingree, Earl S. Young, P. A. Feater, O. M. Gary.

Statement November 15, 1920

RESOURCES

Cash on hand ....$	3,291.28
Due from banks	51,700.87
Checks and drafts on other banks	230.25
Loans and discounts	144,381.46
Overdrafts	417.95
Stocks, bonds, warrants	8,324.81
Banking house, furniture and fixtures	4,941.88
Total ....$	213,288.50

LIABILITIES

Individual deposits subject to check ....$	88,326.63
Savings deposits	4,843.64
Time certificates of deposit	65,601.78
Cashier's checks	4,986.86
Certified checks	500.00
Total deposits	164,258.91
Capital stock paid in	25,000.00
Surplus	2,500.00
Undivided profits, less expenses, interest and taxes paid	1,385.09
Bils, payable, including obligations representing money borrowed	17,144.50
Re-discounts	3,000.00
Total ....$	213,288.50

ELK RIVER

ELK RIVER STATE BANK

A. W. Laird ....President
Andrew Bloom .... Vice President
Robert Haynes ....Cashier

Directors—A. W. Laird, Andrew Bloom, Robert Haynes, John Kendall, Henry Turrish, F. S. Bell.

Statement November 15, 1920

RESOURCES

Cash on hand ....$	12,171.40
Due from banks	66,576.21
Checks and drafts on other banks	344.27
Loans and discounts	87,504.00
Overdrafts	398.89
Stocks, bonds & warrants	51,138.58
Banking house, furniture and fixtures	1,800.00
Total	$219,933.35

LIABILITIES

Individual deposits subject to check ....$	89,431.40
Savings deposits	76,134.11
Demand certificates of deposit	28,807.30
Due to other banks (deposits)	2,815.88
Total deposits	197,188.69
Capital stock paid in	15,000.00
Surplus	3,000.00
Undivided profits, less expenses, interest and taxes paid	4,744.66
Total ....$	$219,933.35

EMMETT

BANK OF EMMETT

D. H. Van Duesen ....President
R. N. Cummings ....Vice President
V. T. Craig ....Cashier
Lauren Dean ....Asst. Cashier

Directors—D. H. Van Dusen, R. N. Cummings, V. T. Craig, Lauren Dean, E. M. Reilly, J. L. Steward.

Statement November 15, 1920

RESOURCES

Cash on hand ....$	12,238.80
Due from banks	98,252.45
Checks and drafts on other banks	10,252.13
Other cash items	3,261.32
Loans and discounts	637,917.69
Stocks, bonds & warrants	54,153.43
Banking house, furniture and fixtures	17,972.65
Other real estate	9,621.94
Other resources — Transit account	2.45
Liberty bonds and Victory notes	72,591.00
Total	$916,263.86

LIABILITIES

Individual deposits subject to check	$466,275.24
Savings deposits	32,692.89
Demand certificates of deposit	74,571.05
Time certificates of deposit	92,060.27
Cashier's checks	20,146.34
Certified checks	7.25
Total deposits	685,753.04
Capital stock paid in	60,000.00
Surplus	25,000.00
Undivided profits, less expenses, interest and taxes paid	9,698.28
Reserved for taxes	7.55
Bills payable, including obligations representing money borrowed	99,000.00
Re-discounts	36,804.99
Total	$916,263.86

FERDINAND

BANK OF FERDINAND
Private Bank

I. N. Canfield .... Cashier

.Statement November 15, 1920

RESOURCES

Cash on hand ....$	1,570.21
Due from banks	5,000.00
Other cash items	57.72
Loans and discounts	57,340.83
Overdrafts	746.66
Banking house, furniture and fixtures	2,400.00
Total ....$	67,115.42

LIABILITIES

Individual deposits subject to check ....$	25,565.70
Time certificates of deposit	18,578.16
Due to other banks	8,029.55
Total deposits	52,173.41
Capital stock paid in	10,000.00
Surplus	2,000.00
Undivided profits, less expenses, interest and taxes	2,942.01
Total ....$	67,115.42

FERDINAND

FERDINAND STATE BANK

E. M. Ehrhardt ....President
H. W. Uhlenkott ....Vice President
F. M. Bieker .... Cashier
E. J. Kinzer ....Asst. Cashier

Directors—E. M. Ehrhardt, H. W. Uhlenkott, F. M. Bieker, Henry Kuther, Fred Enneking.

Statement November 15, 1920

RESOURCES

Cash on hand ....$	3,462.64
Due from banks	10,499.69
Other cash items	91.58
Loans and discounts	78,706.43
Overdrafts	426.64
Stocks, bonds & warrants	16,169.94
Banking house, furniture and fixtures	6,400.00
Total $115,756.92

LIABILITIES

Individual deposits subject to check ....$	28,503.93
Demand certificates of deposit	49.00
Time certificates of deposit	71,391.26
Total deposits	99,944.19
Capital stock paid in	12,500.00
Surplus	2,500.00
Undivided profits, less expenses, interest and taxes paid	812.73
Total $115,756.92

FILER

FARMERS & MERCHANTS BANK

H. H. Schildman ....President
W. A. Shear ....Vice President
A. O. Madland .... Cashier

Directors—H. H. Schildman, W. A. Shear, A. O. Madland, W. W. Taylor, H. J. Hoffman.

Statement November 15, 1920

RESOURCES

Cash on hand ....$	2,949.83
Due from banks	20,806.10
Checks and drafts on other banks	268.84
Loans and discounts	190,789.32
Overdrafts	90.23
Stocks, bonds, warrants	1,229.57
Banking house, furniture and fixtures	6,000.00
U. S. Liberty Bonds	10,800.00
Stock in Fed. Reserve Bk	850.00
Item in transit	78.00
Total ....$	233,861.89

LIABILITIES

Individual deposits subject to check	118,534.26
Demand certs. of deposit..	1,523.95
Time certs. of deposit	53,035.44
Cashier's checks	340.60
Total deposits	173,434.25
Capital stock paid in	25,000.00
Surplus	2,500.00
Undivided profits, less expenses, interest and taxes paid	2,332.64
Bills payable, including obligations representing money borrowed	9,500.00
Re-discounts with Federal Reserve Bank	21,095.00
Total ....$	233,861.89

FRUITLAND

FRUITLAND STATE BANK.

O. E. Bossen .... President
H. R. Boomer .... Vice-Pres.
F. M. Gardner .... Cashier
John L. Towne .... Asst. Cashier
Clare E. Kinsey .... Asst. Cashier

Directors—O. E. Bossen, H. R. Boomer, F. W. Greep, John Rands, Geo. Frank.

Statement November 15, 1920

RESOURCES

Cash on hand ....$	3,302.72
Due from banks	14,705.49
Checks and drafts on other banks	14.50
Other cash items	142.80
Loans and discounts	287,000.66
Overdrafts	11,646.32
Stocks, bonds, warrants	22,946.90
Claims, judgments, etc.	2,500.00
Banking house, furniture and fixtures	7,633.00
Other real estate	1,526.68
Total ....$	341,419.07

LIABILITIES

Individual deposits subject to check	210,085.46
Savings deposits	6,207.12
Time certs. of deposit	84,761.16
Cashier's checks	445.22
Certified checks	2,559.08
Total deposits	304,068.04
Capital stock paid in	25,000.00
Surplus	1,000.00
Undivided profits	1,351.03
Bills payable	10,000.00
Total ....$	341,419.07

GENESEE

FIRST BANK OF GENESEE

A. E. Clarke .... President
N. S. Vollmer .... Vice-Pres.
G. E. Taber .... Cashier
J. M. Tedford .... Asst. Cashier

Directors—A. E. Carke, N. S. Vollmer, G. E. Taber, E. W. Eaves, A. E. Kroutinger.

Statement November 15, 1920

RESOURCES

Cash on hand ....$	8,406.05
Due from banks	7,393.35
Checks and drafts on other banks	307.37
Loans and discounts	349,696.84
Overdrafts	11,882.69
Stocks, bonds, warrants	2,836.99
Banking house, furniture and fixtures	7,436.00
Other real estate	4,000.00
Total ....$	$391,959.29

LIABILITIES

Individual deposits subject to check ....$	$140,989.44
Savings deposits	920.86
Postal Savings deposits	38.55
Time certs. of deposit	195,251.44
Cashier's checks	176.97
Total deposits	337,377.26
Capital stock paid in	15,000.00
Surplus	5,000.00
Undivided profits	9,582.03
Bills payable	25,000.00
Total ....$	$391,959.29

GENESEE

GENESEE EXCHANGE BANK

T. Driscoll .... President
Fred K. Bressler .... Vice-Pres.
C. P. Whalen .... Cashier
D. L. Bressler .... Asst. Cashier

Directors—T. Driscoll, Fred K. Bressler, C. P. Whalen, Leon Follett, W. J. Herman.

Statement November 15, 1920

RESOURCES

Cash on hand ....$	16,791.00
Due from banks	125,533.98
Checks and drafts on other banks	826.78
Other cash items—None.	
Loans and discounts	461,563.49
Overdrafts	2,290.00
Stocks, bonds, warrants	6,200.00
Banking house, furniture and fixtures	12,750.00
Other real estate	2,000.00
Revenue Stamps	52.00
Collection account	29.80
Total ....$	$628,037.05

LIABILITIES

Individual deposits subject to check ....$	$238,369.75
Demand certs. of deposit ..	4,519.49
Time certs .of deposit	331,031.90
Due to other banks (deposits)	14,369.11
Total deposits	588,290.25
Capital stock paid in	25,000.00
Surplus	12,500.00
Undivided profits, less expenses, interest and taxes paid	2,246.80
Total ....$	$628,037.05

GIFFORD

BANK OF GIFFORD

Louis Clark .... President
E. W. Eaves .... Vice-Pres.
F. L. Wicks .... Cashier

Directors—Louis Clark, E. W. Eaves, F. L. Wicks, A. E. Clarke, John P. Vollmer Estate, E. P. Atchison, N. S. Vollmer-Hopkins, S. D. White.

Statement November 15, 1920

RESOURCES

Cash on hand ....$	2,582.87
Due from banks	20,473.29
Other cash items	116.50
Loans and discounts	166,280.13
Overdrafts	1,535.33
Stocks, bonds, warrants	1,500.00
Banking house, furniture and fixtures	600.00
Total ....$	193,088.12

LIABILITIES

Individual deposits subject to check ....$	105,179.20
Demand certs. of deposit ..	11,148.64
Time certs of deposit	37,011.80
Total deposits	153,339.64
Capital stock paid in	10,000.00
Surplus	2,000.00
Undivided profits, less expenses, interest and taxes paid	3,348.48
Bills payable, including obligations representing money borrowed	24,400.00
Total ....$	193,088.12

GLENNS FERRY

GLENNS FERRY BANK

Joseph Rosevear .... President
H. W. Knox .... Vice-Pres.
Ed. M. Clark .... Cashier

Directors—Jos. Rosevear, H. W. Knox, Ed. M. Clark, H. M. Hurbbert, H. W. Knox, Geo. Rosevear, Chas. Walker, J. J. McGinnes.

Statement November 15, 1920

RESOURCES

Cash on hand ....$	19,241.34
Due from banks	100,280.73
Other cash items	110.04
Loans and discounts	214,439.38
Overdrafts	31.01
Stocks, bonds, warrants	102,891.02
Total ....$	436,994.02

LIABILITIES

Individual deposits subject to check ....$	352,552.10
Demand certs. of deposit ..	2,859.14
Time certs. of deposit	42,890.14
Total deposits	398,301.38
Capital stock paid in	20,000.00
Surplus	10,000.00
Undivided profits, less expenses, interest and taxes paid	8,692.64
Total ....$	436,994.02

GOODING

CITIZENS STATE BANK

Geo. W. Wedgewood .... President
W. H. Cannon .... Vice-Pres.
H. J. Leyson .... Cashier
C. L. Miller .... Asst. Cashier
H. J. Leyson, Jr. .... Asst. Cashier

Directors—Geo. W. Wedgewood, W. H. Cannon, H. J. Leyson, C. L. Miller W. T. Robinson.

Statement November 15, 1920

RESOURCES

Cash on hand ....$	3,739.92
Due from banks	76,495.37
Checks and drafts on other banks	1,751.02
Other cash items	3,060.13
Loans and discounts	265,742.96
Overdrafts	298.51
Stocks, bonds, warrants	24,165.30
Banking house, furniture and fixtures	16,386.45
Revenue stamps	66.50
Total ....$	392,506.16

LIABILITIES

Individual deposits subject to check ....$	204,580.36
Savings deposits	3,220.67
Demand certs. of deposit ..	903.00
Time certs. of deposit	54,192.95
Cashier's checks	6,420.00
Certified checks	846.38
Total deposits ....$	270,163.36
Capital stock paid in	25,000.00
Surplus	15,000.00
Undivided profits, less expenses, interest and taxes paid	6,453.80
Reserved for taxes	889.00
Bills payable, including obligations representing money borrowed	75,000.00
Govt. bonds for cert. of deposits	800.00
Total ....$	392,506.16

GRAND VIEW

GRAND VIEW STATE BANK

Russell C. Massey .... President
Chas. E. Blodgett .... Vice-Pres.
J. O. Ball .... Cashier

Directors—Russell C. Massey, Chas. E. Blodgett, J. O. Ball, Chas. Thomson, S. A. Mullenix.

Statement November 15, 1920

RESOURCES

Cash on hand ....$	1,095.27
Due from banks	3,252.16
Checks and drafts on other banks	787.64
Loans and discounts	135,656.52
Overdrafts	790.90
Stocks, bonds, warrants	10,201.39
Banking house, furniture and fixtures	8,200.00
Other real estate	3,200.00
Total	163,183.88

LIABILITIES

Individual deposits subject to check	59,344.18
Time certs. of deposit	18,681.52
Cashier's checks	4,589.16
Total deposits	82,614.85
Capital stock paid in	10,000.00
Surplus fund	5,000.00
Undivided profits, less expenses, interest and taxes paid	2,219.17
Bills payable, including obligations representing money borrowed	10,000.00
Re-discounts	53,349.85
Total	163,183.88

GRANGEVILLE

BANK OF CAMAS PRAIRIE

Frank W. Kettenbach .... President
W. W. Brown .... Vice-Pres.
Frank McGrane .... Vice-Pres.
A. H. Wethrebee .... Cashier
Wm. C. Graham .... Asst. Cashier

Directors — Frank W. Kettenbach;
W. W. Brown, Frank McGrane, Evan
Evans, Milton Freidenrich, A. L. Gil-
keson, A. F. Parker.

Statement November 15, 1920

RESOURCES

Cash on hand ....$ 7,873.48
Due from banks 79,179.08
Checks and drafts on
    other banks 7,519.08
Other cash items 319.72
Loans and discounts 621,545.90
Overdrafts 3,773.46
Stocks, bonds, warrants 75,977.02
Claims, judgments, etc. 4,211.60
Banking house, furniture
    and fixtures 10,500.00
Other real estate 8,388.80
Federal Reserve stock 3,000.00

Total $822,288.14

LIABILITIES

Individual deposits subject
    to check 333,739.18
Savings deposits 1,830.53
Demand certs. of deposit ..   3,767.12
Time certs. of deposit 261,118.95
Certified checks 174.58
Due to other banks (de-
    posits) 9,465.96

Total deposits 610,096.32
Capital stock paid in 50,000.00
Surplus 50,000.00
Undivided profits, less ex-
    penses, interest and
    taxes paid 19,341.82
Re-discounts 92,850.00

Total $822,288.14

GRANGEVILLE

GRANGEVILLE SAVINGS & TRUST COMPANY.

Henry Telcher .... President
Herman von Bargen .... Vice-Pres.
R. H. Russell .... Cashier

Directors—Henry Telcher, Herman
von Bargen; J. A. Bradbury, C. B.
Knorr.

Statement November 15, 1920

RESOURCES

Cash on hand ....$ 4,589.76
Due from banks 16,512.31
Other cash items 2,224.93
Loans and discounts 197,853.84
Stocks, bonds, warrants 9,917.31
Banking house, furniture
    and fixtures 27,500.00
Other real estate 4,690.00
Abstract department 2,000.00

Total $265,288.15

LIABILITIES

Individual deposits subject
    to check 76,121.95
Savings deposits 3,891.95
Demand certs. of deposit ..   100.00
Time certs. of deposit 45,583.61
Cashier's checks 9,585.39

Total deposits $135,282.90
Capital stock paid in 45,000.00
Surplus 2,000.00
Undivided profits, less ex-
    penses, interest and
    taxes paid 4,411.25
Re-discounts 78,589.00
Letters of credit 5.00

Total $265,288.15

HANSEN

BANK OF HANSEN

Laurence Hansen .... President
Chris. Peterson .... Vice-Pres.
A. D. Pollock .... Vice-Pres.
Joy B. Taylor .... Cashier
Leslie Taylor .... Asst. Cashier

Directors—Laurence Hansen, Chris Peterson, A. D. Pollock, Joy B. Taylor, H. M. Vanderpool, Geo. D. Crockett.

Statement November 15, 1920

RESOURCES

Cash on hand ....$	5,963.38
Due from banks	8,647.93
Loans and discounts	360,530.24
Overdrafts	2,988.69
Stocks, bonds, warrants	9,577.43
Claims, judgments, etc.	1,223.55
Banking house, furniture and fixtures	7,227.65
Stock Fed. Reserve Bank	900.00
Total $397,058.87	

LIABILITIES

Individual deposits subject to check $151,859.94	
Time certs. of deposit	59,312.55
Cashier's checks	2,704.95
Total deposits $213,877.44	
Capital stock paid in	25,000.00
Surplus	5,000.00
Undivided profits, less expenses, interest and taxes paid	3,280.00
Bills payable	33,850.00
Re-discounts, Federal Reserve bank	114,126.99
Other liabilities	1,924.41
Total $397,058.87	

HARRISON

FIRST BANK OF HANSEN

J. F. Pollock .... President
Horace Sampson .... Vice-Pres.
E. O. Cathcart .... Cashier

Directors—J. F. Pollock, Horace Sampson, E. O. Cathcart, A. Cooskia, W. S. Bridgeman.

Statement November 15, 1920

RESOURCES

Bills Receivable (notes) $145,192.90	
Overdrafts	7.04
Bonds and warrants	19,100.71
Liberty Bonds	11,450.00
Banking house	3,000.00
Furniture and fixtures	2,400.00
Other real estate (corner lot)	508.38
Cash and due from banks..	106,871.94
Total $288,530.97	

LIABILITIES

Capital stock ....$	15,000.00
Surplus and undivided profits	7,674.92
Liberty Bonds, borrowed of officers	6,800.00
Deposits $259,056.05	
Total $288,530.97	

HAZELTON

HAZELTON STATE BANK

E. W. Rieman .... President
H. Eyers .... Vice-Pres.
H. E. Gundlefinger .... Cashier
W. L. Mitchell .... Asst. Cashier

Directors—E. W. Rieman, H. Eyers, H. E. Gundlefinger, W. S. Dunn, S. S. Brooks, J. B. Barlow, Wm. Lockwood.

Statement November 15, 1920

RESOURCES

Cash on hand ....$	6,067.14
Due from banks	35,150.78
Checks and drafts on other banks	507.58
Other cash items	297.14
Loans and discounts	170,728.35
Overdrafts	177.92
Stocks, bonds & warrants	26,021.39
Banking house, furniture and fixtures	14,894.80
Total ....$	253,845.10

LIABILITIES

Individual deposits subject to check ....$	136,555.12
Savings deposits	4,981.39
Demand certificates of deposit	3,516.00
Time certificates of deposit	50,543.40
Cashier's checks	11,428.75
Certified checks	200.00
Total deposits	207,224.66
Capital stock paid in	25,000.00
Surplus	5,700.00
Undivided profits, less expenses, interest and taxes paid	920.44
Bills payable, including obligations representing money borrowed	15,000.00
Total ....$	253,845.10

HEYBURN

HEYBURN STATE BANK

F. M. Snyder ....President
J. J. Connor ....Vice President
A. B. Campbell ....Cashier

Directors—F. M. Snyder, J. J. Connor, W. H. Disney, Geo. E. Schroeder, Carry M. Snyder.

Statement November 15, 1920

RESOURCES

Cash on hand ....$	1,594.76
Due from banks	6,185.63
Other cash items	2.36
Loans and discounts	124,525.60
Overdrafts	247.42
Stocks, bonds & warrants	13,298.70
Banking house, furniture and fixtures	9,500.00
Items in transit	635.92
Total ....$	155,990.39

LIABILITIES

Individual deposits ....$	68,887.96
Demand certificates	1,360.94
Time certificates	19,990.02
Total deposits	90,238.92
Capital stock	10,000.00
Surplus	10,000.00
Undivided profits	1,762.02
Bills payable	33,680.74
Re-discounts	10,020.00
Other liabilities	288.71
Total ....$	155,990.39

HOLLISTER

BANK OF HOLLISTER

W. H. Craven .... President
Henry Jones ....Vice President
A. F. Craven ....Cashier

Directors—W. H. Craven, Henry Jones, A. F. Craven, J. B. Rice, J. M. Bratten.

Statement November 15, 1920

RESOURCES

Cash on hand ....$	4,159.89
Due from banks	7,633.36
Checks and drafts on other banks	230.60
Other cash items	None
Loans and discounts	100,479.00
Overdrafts	137.03
Stocks, bonds & warrants	5,166.37
Premium on bonds	None
Claims, judgments, etc.	856.60
Banking house, furniture and fixtures	12,500.00
Other real estate	4,829.56
Other resources	None
Expense excess of earnings	None
Total ....$	135,992.41

LIABILITIES

Individual deposits ....$	49,751.94
Time certificates	35,612.74
Cashier's checks	589.83
Total deposits	85,954.51
Capital stock paid in	20,000.00
Surplus	5,000.00
Undivided profits	37.90
Bills payable	25,000.00
Total ....$	135,992.41

HOMEDALE

FIRST BANK OF HOMEDALE

J. R. Blackaby .... President
O. K. Blackaby .... Vice-Pres.
J. P. Kropp .... Cashier

Directors—J. R. Blackaby O. K. Blackaby, J. P. Kropp, R. W. Vanderhoof, C. M. Sutton.

Statement November 15, 1920

RESOURCES

Cash on hand ....$	1,207.36
Due from banks	12,632.74
Other cash items	245.37
Loans and discounts	131,260.66
Overdrafts	.09
Stocks, bonds, warrants	5,500.00
Banking house, furniture and fixtures	7,821.22
Over and short	99.19
Total ....$	158,766.63

LIABILITIES

Individual deposits subject to check ....$	72,269.18
Time certs. of deposit	39,233.90
Cashier's checks	1,166.30
Total deposits ....$	112,669.38
Capital stock paid in	25,000.00
Undivided profits, less expenses, interest and taxes paid	2,508.05
Re-discounts	18,123.95
Depreciation bond account	465.25
Total ....$	158,766.63

HORSESHOE BEND	IDAHO FALLS
FIRST STATE BANK	**ANDERSON BROS. BANK**

J. A. Lippincott .... President	G. G. Wright .... President
F. W. Clarkson .... Vice-Pres.	Jas. E. Steele .... Vice-Pres.
T. S. Whitsides .... Cashier	M. M. Hitt .... Cashier
	G. B. Willsey .... Asst. Cashier
Directors—J. A. Lippincott, F. W. Clarkson, T. S. Whitesides, Elmer Davis, Geo. E. Hobson.	*Directors*—G. G. Wright, James E. Steele, M. M. Hitt, E. C. Barnes, Christian Anderson.
Statement November 15, 1920	Statement November 15, 1920

RESOURCES

Cash on hand ....$	3,272.08	Cash on hand ....$	15,524.25
Due from banks	9,819.57	Due from banks	198,800.20
Checks and drafts on other banks	333.35	Checks and drafts on other banks	41,868.11
Other cash items	302.53	Other cash items	222.69
Loans and discounts	17,943.00	Loans and discounts	2,366,062.38
Overdrafts	1.25	Overdrafts	6,481.72
Stocks, bonds, warrants	7,781.53	Stocks, bonds, warrants	99,183.59
Claims, judgments, etc.	383.40	Bonneville Co. bonds	125,000.00
Banking house, furniture and fixtures	9,756.18	Liberty Bonds	527,800.00
		Banking house, furniture and fixtures	18,250.00
		Other real estate	47,000.00
		Stock in Fed. Reserve Bk	15,150.00
Total ....$	49,592.89	Total ....$	3,461,342.94

LIABILITIES

Individual deposits subject to check ....$	28,317.29	Individual deposits subject to check	900,062.59
Time certs. of deposit	2,424.46	Time certs. of deposit	507,548.66
Cashier's checks	1,165.25	Cashier's checks	26,154.97
		Certified checks	467.95
		Due to other banks (deposits)	25,690.80
		Dividends unpaid	1,106.25
Total deposits	31,907.00	Total deposits	1,461,031.22
Capital stock paid in	15,000.00	Capital stock paid in	100,000.00
Surplus	2,000.00	Surplus	120,000.00
Undivided profits, less expenses, interest and taxes paid	685.89	Undivided profits, less expenses, interest and taxes paid	51,948.04
		Bills payable, including obligations representing money borrowed	526,000.00
		Re-discounts	810,563.00
		Increase Capital Stock account	391,800.68
Total ....$	49,592.89	Total ....$	3,461,342.94

IDAHO FALLS

FARMERS & MERCHANTS BANK

F. C. Osgood .... President
O. K. Wilbur .... Vice-Pres.
A. T. Shane .... Vice-Pres.
C. A. Spath .... Cashier
Victor Austin .... Asst. Cashier
O. W. Ellingson .... Asst. Cashier
Directors—E. W. Rowles, A. B. Anderson, Chas. E. Kaiser, John W. Hart, F. C. Osgood, O. K. Wilbur, A. T. Shane, C. A. Spath.

Statement November 15, 1920

RESOURCES
Cash on hand ....$ 20,680.55
Due from banks 168,335.28
Checks and drafts on
  other banks 46,031.40
Loans and discounts 1,308,468.97
Stocks, bonds, warrants 161,226.22
U. S. Liberty Loan and
  Victory Bonds 150,450.00
Banking house, furniture
  and fixtures 55,000.00
Other real estate 3,800.00
Fed. Reserve Bank stock .. 5,250.00

Total $1,919,242.42

LIABILITIES
Individual deposits subject
  to check $668,391.75
Savings deposits 137,611.99
Demand certs. of deposit .. 10,006.32
Time certs. of deposit 121,868.04
Cashier's checks 25,109.67
Certified checks 349.43
Due to other banks (de-
  posits) 34,479.21

Total deposits 997,816.41
Capital stock paid in 150,000.00
Surplus 30,000.00
Undivided profits, less expenses, interest and
  taxes paid 8,905.25
Bills payable, including
  obligations representing
  money borrowed 315,000.00
Re-discounts 417,520.76

Total $1,919,242.42

IDAHO FALLS

THE STATE BANK

V. K. Tuggle .... President
C. G. Peck .... Vice-Pres.
C. C. Whipple .... Cashier
C. I. Canfield .... Asst. Cashier

Directors—V. K. Tuggle, C. G. Peck, C. C. Whipple, L. A. Hartert, J. I. Hubble.

Statement November 15, 1920

RESOURCES
Cash on hand ....$ 26,398.97
Due from Banks 70,870.69
Checks and drafts on
  other banks 72,539.20
Other cash items 23,348.31
Loans and discounts 1,050,968.55
Overdrafts—None.
Stocks, bonds, warrants 141,227.86
Premium on bonds—none.
Claims, judgm'ts, etc., none
Banking house, furniture
  and fixtures 30,027.50
Other real estate 7,049.44
Other resources—none.
Expenses in excess of
  earnings 1,856.06

Total $1,424,286.58

LIABILITIES
Individual deposits 639,776.34
Savings deposits 29,000.85
Postal Sav. dep.—none.
Demand cert. dep.—none.
Time certs. of deposit 87,034.03
Cashier's checks 29,836.35
Certified checks 13,125.94
Due to other banks (de-
  posits) 37,827.67
Dividends unpaid—none.

Total deposits 836,601.18
Capital stock paid in 100,000.00
Surplus 15,000.00
Undivided profits, less expenses, interest and
  and taxes paid ....
Res. for taxes—none.
Bills payable, including
  obligations representing
  money borrowed 345,000.00
Re-discounts 98,285.40
Other liabilities, customer's bond deposit acct. .. 29,400.00

Total $1,424,286.58

JULIAETTA

BANK OF JULIAETTA

E. W. Porter .... President
John L. Woody .... Vice-Pres.

Directors—E. W. Porter, John L. Woody, W. S. Cox, Walter Clark.

Statement November 15, 1920

RESOURCES

Cash on hand ....$	6,276.75
Due from banks	34,361.21
Loans and discounts	119,379.82
Overdrafts	19.87
Stocks, bonds, warrants	4,600.00
Banking house, furniture and fixtures	7,300.00
Other real estate	1,230.00
Other resources	109.20
Total $173,276.85	

LIABILITIES

Individual deposits subject to check	87,598.62
Time certs. of deposit	42,764.75
Cashier's checks	6,495.36
Total deposits $136,858.73	
Capital stock paid in	15,000.00
Surplus	4,500.00
Undivided profits, less expenses, interest and taxes paid	1,918.12
Bills payable, including obligations representing money borrowed	15,000.00
Total $173,276.85	

KAMIAH

CLEARWATER VALLEY STATE BANK

C. J. Johnson .... President
Willis Turner .... Vice-Pres.
Geo. M. Robertson .... Cashier
I. W. Robertson .... Asst. Cashier

Directors—C. J. Johnson, Willis Turner, Geo. M. Robertson, L. B. George, Guy Dissmore, L. F. Horning, G. O. Harvey.

Statement November 15, 1920

RESOURCES

Cash on hand ....$	6,226.14
Due from banks	13,110.88
Loans and discounts	22,435.00
Stocks, bonds, warrants	10.00
Banking house, furniture and fixtures	5,524.90
Expenses in excess of earnings	1,219.05
Total ....$ 48,525.97	

LIABILITIES

Individual deposits subject to check ....$	21,635.02
Demand certs. of deposit ..	500.00
Time certs. of deposit	430.15
Cashier's checks	960.80
Total deposits	23,525.97
Capital stock paid in	25,000.00
Total ....$ 48,525.97	

KAMIAH

STATE BANK OF KAMIAH

Geo. H. Waterman .... President
J. F. Bridwell .... Vice-Pres.
Ward L. Dempsey .... Cashier
Leslie L. Roth .... Asst. Cashier

Directors—Geo. H. Waterman, J. F. Bridwell, Ward L. Dempsey, J. F. Pomeroy, C. H. Works.

Statement November 15, 1920

RESOURCES

Cash on hand ....$	8,486.95
Due from banks	12,477.03
Checks and drafts on other banks	30.24
Loans and Discounts	344,926.59
Overdrafts	836.42
Stocks, bonds, warrants	1,444.85
Banking house, furniture and fixtures	9,192.65
Other real estate	1,655.46
U. S. Revenue Stamps	283.30
Checks and drafts on other banks outside of city in transit	4,673.75
Total ....$	384,007.24

LIABILITIES

Individual deposits subject to check ....$	110,398.03
Savings deposits	6,781.57
Demand certs. of deposit ..	32,100.56
Time certs. of deposit	120,667.64
Certified checks	300.00
Due to other banks (deposits)	12,954.57
Total deposits	283,202.37
Capital stock paid in	25,000.00
Surplus	5,000.00
Undivided profits, less expenses, interest and taxes paid	804.87
Bills payable, including obligations representing money borrowed	70,000.00
Total ....$	384,007.24

KELLOGG

FIRST STATE BANK

W. W. Papesh .... President
O. M. Green .... Vice-Pres.
W. O. Straight .... Cashier
Loyd McDougall .... Asst. Cashier

Directors—W. W. Papesh, O. M. Green, W. O. Straight, Geo. F. Bitner, D. W. Peeples, C. W. Miller, C. H. Baker, T. R. Mason.

Statement November 15, 1920

RESOURCES

Cash on hand ....$	18,856.09
Due from banks	76,634.13
Checks and drafts on other banks	5,654.39
Loans and discounts	275,545.59
Overdrafts	35.12
Stocks, bonds, warrants :...	96,323.14
Banking house, furniture and fixtures	18,650.00
Other real estate	5,754.35
Total ....$	497,452.81

LIABILITIES

Individual deposits subject to check ....$	253,925.96
Savings deposits	124,841.25
Postal Savings deposits	5,125.68
Demand certs. of deposit ..	79.80
Time certs. of deposit	54,648.56
Cashier's checks	2,490.63
Certified checks	3.20
Due to other banks (deposits)	90.92
Dividends unpaid	35.00
Total deposits ....$	441,241.00
Capital stock paid in	40,000.00
Surplus	8,000.00
Undivided profits, less expenses, interest and taxes paid	8,211.81
Total ....$	497,452.81

KENDRICK

FARMERS BANK

A. E. Clarke .... President
E. P. Atchison .... Vice-Pres.
M. B. McConnell .... Cashier

Directors—E. W. Eaves, E. E. Tupper, N. S. Vollmer-Hopkins, A. E. Clarke, E. P. Atchison, M. B. McConnell.

Statement November 15, 1920

RESOURCES

Cash on hand ....$	7,533.71
Due from banks	18,431.60
Checks and drafts on other banks	446.19
Other cash items	204.20
Loans and discounts	181,041.32
Overdrafts	434.67
Stocks, bonds, warrants	7,007.14
Banking house, furniture and fixtures	10,331.03
Other real estate	1,000.35
Total ....$	226,430.21

LIABILITIES

Individual deposits subject to check ....$	87,086.22
Savings deposits	24,447.71
Postal savings deposits	565.50
Time certs. of deposit	60,194.01
Cashier's checks	5,732.69
Total deposits	178,026.13
Capital stock paid in	15,000.00
Surplus	3,000.00
Undivided profits, less expenses, interest and taxes paid	5,404.08
Bills payable, including obligations representing money borrowed	25,000.00
Total ....$	226,430.21

KENDRICK

KENDRICK STATE BANK

Martin V. Thomas .... President
K. D. Ingle .... Vice-Pres.
E. W. Lutz .... Cashier
Leo C. Raaberg .... Asst. Cashier

Directors—Martin V. Thomas, K. D. Ingle, E. W. Lutz, A. Galloway, H. B. Lutz.

Statement November 15, 1920

RESOURCES

Cash on hand ....$	7,146.77
Due from banks	27,388.12
Checks and drafts on other banks	436.85
Other cash items	127.18
Loans and discounts	205,462.97
Overdrafts	300.54
Stocks, bonds, warrants	32,195.54
Banking house, furniture and fixtures	7,592.50
Other real estate	2,150.00
Total ....$	282,800.47

LIABILITIES

Individual deposits subject to check ....$	146,536.96
Savings deposits	32,147.53
Time certs. of deposit	53,618.84
Cashier's checks	8,967.95
Total deposits	241,271.28
Capital stock paid in	15,000.00
Surplus	5,000.00
Undivided profits, less expenses, interest and taxes paid	11,529.19
Bills payable, including obligations representing money borrowed	10,000.00
Total ....$	282,800.47

KIMBERLY

BANK OF KIMBERLY

Henry Jones .... President
H. P. Larsen .... Vice-Pres.
W. H. Turner .... Cashier
J. F. Denham .... Asst. Cashier

Directors—Henry Jones, H. P. Larsen, A. B. Norton, C. T. Brown, W. E. Lewis, A. J. Fuller, J. B. Rice.

Statement November 15, 1920

RESOURCES

Cash on hand ....$	6,473.67
Due from banks	28,433.04
Checks and drafts on other banks	5,313.60
Other cash items	550.62
Loans and discounts	333,936.59
Stocks, bonds, warrants	26,586.51
Banking house, furniture and fixtures	17,613.50
Expenses in excess of earnings	189.41
Total ....$	$419,096.94

LIABILITIES

Individual deposits subject to check	$154,579.18
Time certs. of deposit	135,166.13
Cashier's checks	2,175.90
Total deposits	291,921.21
Capital stock paid in	35,000.00
Surplus	13,500.00
Reserved for bond depreciation	300.00
Bills payable, including obligations representing money borrowed	25,900.00
Re-discounts	51,375.73
U. S. Bond Certificates	1,100.00
Total ....$	$419,096.94

KOOSKIA

STATE BANK OF KOOSKIA

Geo. H. Waterman .... President
F. E. Quist............ V.-Pres & Cashier
L. H. Cox .... Asst. Cashier

Directors—Geo. H. Waterman, F. E. Quist, C. H. Weeks, N. E. Whiting, F. A. Quist.

Statement November 15, 1920

RESOURCES

Cash on hand ....$	5,929.49
Due from banks	21,975.01
Other cash items	98.75
Loans and discounts	229,058.52
Overdrafts	567.92
Stocks, bonds, warrants	5,772.50
Banking house, furniture and fixtures	5,818.80
Other real estate	1,558.77
Total ....$	$270,779.76

LIABILITIES

Individual deposits subject to check	$140,816.77
Savings deposits	3,447.29
Demand certs. of deposit	8,618.69
Time certs. of deposit	99,927.92
Certified checks	75.00
Total deposits	$252,885.67
Capital stock paid in	10,000.00
Surplus	6,000.00
Undivided profits, less expenses, interest and taxes paid	1,894.09
Total ....$	$270,779.76

KUNA

KUNA STATE BANK.

F. I. Newhouse .... President
J. A. Martin .... Vice-Pres.
L. A. Kalbus .... Cashier

Directors—F. I. Newhouse J. A. Martin, L. M. Beal, C. D. Newhouse.

Statement November 15, 1920

RESOURCES

Cash on hand ....$ 4,598.43
Due from banks 9,294.82
Other cash items 239.52
Loans and discounts 183,121.28
Overdrafts 1,755.27
Stocks, bonds, warrants 19,318.88
Claims, judgments, etc. 100.00
Banking house, furniture
  and fixtures 4,687.70
Fed. Reserve Bank stock 750.00

Total $223,865.90

LIABILITIES

Individual deposits subject
  to check $102,061.93
Time certs. of deposit 17,339.03
Cashier's checks 4,401.76

Total deposits $123,802.72
Capital stock paid in 25,000.00
Surplus 1,250.00
Undivided profits, less expenses, interest and
  taxes paid 516.72
Re-discounts 68,147.68
U. S. Bonds deposited 2,400.00
Other liabilities 2,748.78

Total $223,865.90

LAPWAI

FORT LAPWAI STATE BANK

J. A. Schultz .... President
J. M. Schultz .... Vice-Pres.
Fred J. Schultz .... Cashier

Directors—J. A. Schultz, J. M. Schultz, Fred J. Schultz, M. G. Schultz, Harry J. Schultz.

Statement November 15, 1920

RESOURCES

Cash on hand ....$ 1,406.27
Due from banks 11,391.29
Other cash items 58.44
Loans and discounts 88,794.43
Overdrafts 65.78
Stocks, bonds, warrants 1,025.17
Furniture and fixtures 3,000.00
Other real estate 7,633.65

Total $113,375.03

LIABILITIES

Individual deposits subject
  to check ....$ 64,962.61
Demand certs. of deposit .. 5,693.89
Time certs. of deposit 16,976.69
Certified checks 121.78

Total deposits ....$ 87,754.97
Capital stock 10,000.00
Surplus 10,000.00
Undivided profits 5,620.06

Total $113,375.03

LAVA HOT SPRINGS

LAVA HOT SPRINGS STATE BANK

D. H. Evans .... President
W. R. Godfrey .... Vice-Pres.
D. T. Pilchard .... Cashier

Directors—D. H. Evans, W. R. Godfrey, D. T. Pilchard, Truxton Rainey, F. C. Coffin.

Statement November 15, 1920

RESOURCES

Cash on hand ....$	2,062.40
Due from banks	5,465.76
Other cash items	140.00
Loans and discounts	135,887.03
Stocks, bonds, warrants	11,930.80
Banking house, furniture and fixtures	8,400.00
Other real estate	6,600.00
Expenses in excess of earnings	501.44
Total ....$	170,987.43

LIABILITIES

Individual deposits subject to check ....$	80,414.76
Savings deposits	5,078.96
Demand certs. of deposit ..	826.89
Time certs. of deposit	7,361.00
Cashier's checks	3,325.28
Bond certs. of deposit	2,150.00
Total deposits	99,156.89
Capital stock paid in	25,000.00
Surplus	5,000.00
Bills payable, including obligations representing money borrowed	9,100.00
Re-discounts	26,086.75
Other liabilities	6,643.79
Total ....$	170,987.43

LEADORE

LEMHI VALLEY BANK

Morris H. Cottom .... President
Arthur Damschen .... Vice-Pres.
A. M. Baukel .... Cashier

Directors—Morris H. Cottom, Arthur Damschen, A. M. Baukel, E. M. Yearian, E. C. Ross.

Statement November 15, 1920

RESOURCES

Cash on hand ....$	2,013.66
Due from banks	13,906.04
Other cash items	100.00
Loans and discounts	131,763.29
Overdrafts	377.07
Stocks, bonds, warrants	5,187.50
Claims, judgments, etc.	932.22
Banking house, furniture and fixtures	1,600.00
Other real estate	1,800.00
Total ....$	157,679.78

LIABILITIES

Individual deposits subject to check ....$	72,090.99
Time certs. of deposit	44,066.38
Cashier's checks	3,415.61
Total deposits	119,572.98
Capital stock paid in	25,000.00
Surplus	2,750.00
Undivided profits, less expenses, interest and taxes paid	356.80
Bills payable, including obligations representing money borrowed	10,000.00
Total ....$	157,679.78

LEWISTON

IDAHO TRUST COMPANY

Wm. Thomson .... President
J. B. Morris .... Vice-Pres.
R. C. Beach .... Cashier
Arnold P. Henzell .... Asst. Cashier

Directors—Wm. Thompson, J. B. Morris, R. C. Beach, P. J. Miller, T. F. Wren, E. A. Cox, E. L. Alford, James Lambert, J. K. McCormack.

Statement November 15, 1920

RESOURCES

Cash on hand ....$	2,549.45
Due from banks	6,583.16
Loans and discounts	112,267.28
Stocks, bonds, warrants	17,436.66
Furniture and fixtures	2,408.30
Other real estate	20,957.17
Total $162,202.02	

LIABILITIES

Individual deposits subject to check ....$	30,987.84
Savings deposits	25,695.55
Demand certs. of deposit ..	16,847.20
Time certs. of deposit	1,390.66
Certified checks	6.00
Trust funds	10,484.67
Total deposits	85,411.92
Capital stock paid in	50,000.00
Surplus	10,000.00
Undivided profits, less expenses, interest and taxes paid	9,290.10
Bills payable, including obligations representing money borrowed	7,500.00
Total $162,202.02	

McCAMMON

McCAMMON STATE BANK

C. A. Valentine .... President
E. W. Riebe ....Vice President
E. C. Goodwin ....Cashier

Directors—C. A. Valentine, E. W. Riebe, E. C. Goodwin, W. B. Wright, David Armstrong.

Statement November 15, 1920

RESOURCES

Cash on hand ....$	3,184.44
Other cash items	539.66
Loans and discounts	134,249.91
Overdrafts .... None	
Stocks, bonds & warrants	59,570.56
Banking house, furniture and fixtures	2,500.00
Other real estate	750.00
Total $200,794.57	

LIABILITIES

Individual deposits subject to check ....$	63,346.46
Savings deposits	·14,962.90
Time certificates of deposit	17,859.07
Cashier's checks	4,492.04
Dividends unpaid	4.00
Total deposits	100,664.47
Capital stock paid in	15,000.00
Surplus	5,000.00
Undivided profits, less expenses, interest and taxes paid	866.27
Bills payable, including obligations representing money borrowed	62,850.00
Othed liabilities— Liberty bond cert. of deposit	5,150.00
Due to banks—O. D.	11,263.83
Total $200,794.57	

MACKAY

W. G. JENKINS & COMPANY, BANKERS

J. H. Greene .... President
C. C. Davidson ....Vice President
D. T. Archbold ....Cashier
Mrs. M. Thomas ....Asst. Cashier

Directors—J. H. Greene, C. C. Davidson, D. V. Archbold, D. W. Standrod, D. L. Evans, C. W. Berryman.

Statement November 15, 1920

RESOURCES

Cash on hand ....$	12,506.21
Due from banks	117,368.65
Checks and drafts on other banks	531.72
Other cash items	260.36
Loans and discounts	264,107.98
Stocks, bonds & warrants	95,875.04
Claims, judgments, etc.....	10,965.25
Banking house, furniture and fixtures	5,350.00
Other real estate	5,000.00
Other resources	626.35
Total ....$	512,591.56

LIABILITIES

Individual deposits subject to check ....$	195,504.47
Savings deposits	146,243.60
Time certificates of deposit	58,896.23
Cashier's checks	2,014.03
Certified checks	27.85
Dividends unpaid	3,000.00
Total deposits	405,686.18
Capital stock paid in	50,000.00
Surplus	10,000.00
Undivided profits, less expenses, interest and taxes paid	6,405.38
Reserved for taxes	500.00
Bills payable, including money borrowed	40,000.00
Total ....$	512,591.56

MALAD

J. N. IRELAND & COMPANY, BANKERS

D. L. Evans .... President
D. L. Evans, Jr. ....Vice President
W. R. Evans .... Cashier
E. P. Jones ....Asst. Cashier

Directors—D. W. Standrod, G. L. Jenkins, Mary E. Evans, D. L. Evans, D. L. Evans, Jr., W. R. Evans.

Statement November 15, 1920

RESOURCES

Cash on hand ....$	15,121.22
Due from banks	68,895.65
Checks and drafts on other banks	1,968.47
Other cash items	696.76
Loans and discounts	408,110.80
Overdrafts	1,269.96
Stocks, bonds & warrants	22,091.21
Furniture and fixtures	1,500.00
Other real estate	561.35
U. S. Liberty bonds owned	87,870.71
Total ....$	608,086.63

LIABILITIES

Individual deposits subject to check ....$	352,232.62
Demand certificates of deposit	3,280.64
Time certificates of deposit	76,678.34
Total deposits	422,191.60
Capital stock paid in	40,000.00
Surplus	12,500.00
Undivided profits, less expenses, interest and taxes paid	12,070.96
Reserved for taxes	1,324.07
Bills payable, including obligations representing money borrowed	110,000.00
Total ....$	608,086.63

MAY

UNION CENTRAL BANK

Minor A. Brown ....President
Ed. Mulvania ....Vice President
Geo. W. Meitzler ....Cashier

Directors—Minor A. Brown, Ed. Mulvania, Geo. W. Meitzler, G. B. Quarles, S. F. Horn.

Statement November 15, 1920

RESOURCES

Cash on hand ....$	2,355.09
Due from banks	19,309.06
Other cash items	915.00
Loans and discounts	84,734.88
Overdrafts	4.02
Stocks, bonds & warrants	11,000.00
Banking house, furniture and fixtures	6,600.00
Interest earned not collected	3,216.79
Total $128,134.84	

LIABILITIES

Individual deposits subject to check ....$	60,123.57
Demand certificates of deposit	5,415.41
Cashier's checks	7.81
Due to other banks	25.41
Total deposits	65,572.20
Capital stock paid in	30,000.00
Surplus	2,500.00
Undivided profits, less expenses, interest and taxes paid	674.53
Bills payable, including obligations representing money borrowed	8,500.00
Re-discounts	17,051.88
Profit account	3,216.79
Suspense account	619.44
Total $128,134.84	

MENAN

JEFFERSON STATE BANK

John W. Hart ....President
C. A. Smith, Jr. ....Vice President
A. S. Green .... Cashier

Directors—F. J. Hagenbarth, J. S. Harrop, P. B. Ellsworth, Jno. W. Hart, C. A. Smith, Jr.

Statement November 15, 1920

RESOURCES

Cash on hand ....$	1,619.39
Due from banks	57,104.14
Other cash items	965.78
Overdrafts	None
Loans and discounts	166,195.80
Stocks, bonds & warrants	12,670.52
Banking house, furniture and fixtures	7,339.44
Other resources, Federal Reserve stock	750.00
Total $246,645.07	

LIABILITIES

Individual deposits subject to check ....$	104,032.77
Savings deposits	964.98
Time certificates of deposit	12,571.47
Cashier's checks	1,764.02
Due to other banks (deposits)	7,484.73
Total deposits	126,817.97
Capital stock paid in	25,000.00
Surplus	2,500.00
Undivided profits, less expenses, interest and taxes paid	426.89
Reserved for taxes	248.36
Bills payable, including obligations representing money borrowed	36,879.00
Re-discounts	54,772.85
Total $246,645.07	

MERIDIAN

MERIDIAN STATE BANK

F. I. Newhouse ....President
J. W. Hudson ....Vice President
A. D. Stanton .... Cashier

Directors—F. I. Newhouse, J. W. Hudson, A. D. Stanton, C. D. Newhouse, Wm. Goodall.

Statement November 15, 1920

RESOURCES

Loans and discounts $216,821.87	
Bonds and securities	1,375.86
Stock in Federal Reserve Bank	850.00
Furniture and fixtures	2,260.00
Real estate	2,840.00
Overdrafts	960.22
Cash and exchange	22,658.83
Total $247,766.78	

LIABILITIES

Individual deposits subject to check $148,240.46	
Savings deposits	29,632.48
Time certificates of deposit	24,756.18
Cashier's checks	673.72
Total deposits	203,302.84
Capital stock paid in..........	25,000.00
Surplus	3,000.00
Undivided profits, less expenses, and taxes paid....	3,356.55
Re-discounts	7,450.00
Due to other banks	5,657.39
Total $247,766.78	

MIDDLETON

STATE BANK OF MIDDLETON

W. T. Plowhead ....President
P. A. Watkins ....Vice President
R. H. Miller ....Vice President
G. C. Painter ....Cashier
Lela D. Painter ....Asst. Cashier

Directors—Peter Neth, Geo. Oylear, Ed. D. Barney, H. C. Flint, W. T. Plowhead, P. A. Watkins.

Statement November 15, 1920

RESOURCES

Cash on hand ....$ 2,438.60	
Due from banks	29,084.51
Loans and discounts	151,426.16
Stocks, bonds, warrants	34,473.76
Banking house, furniture and fixtures	5,500.00
Other real estate	2,000.00
Total $224,923.03	

LIABILITIES

Individual deposits subject to check $109,782.91	
Savings deposits	8,523.75
Time certificates of deposit	53,015.40
Cashier's checks	500.00
Total deposits	171,822.06
Capital stock paid in	10,000.00
Surplus	3,000.00
Undivided profits, less expenses, interest and taxes paid	5,509.97
Bills payable, including obligations representing money borrowed	34,600.00
Total $224,923.03	

MIDVALE

BANK OF WASHINGTON COUNTY

A. B. Anderson ....President
Geo. Stephens .... Vice President
J. H. Rodgers ....Cashier
H. J. Devaney ....Asst. Cashier

Directors—A. B. Anderson, Geo. Stephens, J. H. Rodgers, Emma B. Elwell, J. W. Stippich, A. A. Seay, Geo. Phillips, J. L. Gilmore.

Statement November 15, 1920

RESOURCES

Cash on hand (lawful money of the United States ....$	4,206.26
Due from banks	29,027.97
Checks and drafts on other banks	1,744.19
Other cash items	1,906.21
Loans and discounts	269,674.46
Overdrafts, secured and unsecured	418.90
Warrants, judgments, etc.	25.00
Banking house, furniture and fixtures	11,300.00
Other real estate	6,078.44
Total ....$	324,381.43

LIABILITIES

Individual deposits, subject to check ....$	173,715.25
Demand certificates of deposit	273.17
Time certificates of deposit	82,148.89
Total deposits ....$	256,137.31
Capital stock paid in	25,000.00
Surplus fund	25,000.00
Undivided profits, less expenses, interest and taxes paid	3,244.12
Bills payable, including obligations representing money borrowed	15,000.00
Total ....$	324,381.43

MONTOUR

FARMERS AND STOCKGROWERS BANK

F. I. Newhouse ....President
A. D. Stanton ....Vice President
I. W. Stoddard ....Cashier

Directors—F. I. Newhouse, A. D. Stanton, I. W. Stoddard, C. D. Newhouse, Harry Sweet.

Statement November 15th, 1920.

RESOURCES

Cash on hand and due from banks ....$	26,730.16
Loans and discounts	146,667.69
Overdrafts	60.95
Stocks, bonds & warrants	38,314.94
Banking house, furniture and fixtures	4,300.00
Transit account	864.67
Total ....$	216,938.61

LIABILITIES

Individual deposits subject to check ....$	103,701.31
Liberty bond deposits	26,850.00
Time certificates of deposit	19,908.34
Cashier's checks	1,313.66
Total deposits	151,773.31
Capital stock paid in	25,000.00
Surplus	850.00
Undivided profits, less expenses, and taxes paid....	691.96
Bills payable, including obligations representing money borrowed	5,000.00
Re-discounts	33,623.34
Total ....$	216,938.61

MONTPELIER

BANK OF MONTPELIER

G. C. Gray ....President
A. D. Gray ....Vice President
Richard Groo ....Cashier

Directors—G. C. Gray, A. D. Gray, Richard Groo, F. D. Gray, C. G. Groo,

Statement November 15th, 1920.

RESOURCES

Cash on hand ....$	11,174.47
Due from banks	77,697.43
Checks and drafts on other banks	2,593.75
Loans and discounts	440,726.56
Overdrafts	1,488.55
Stocks, bonds, warrants	27,020.09
Banking house, furniture and fixtures	24,500.00
Other resources	872.76
Total	$586,055.61

LIABILITIES

Individual deposits subject to check	$209,160.83
Savings deposits	39,062.58
Demand certs. of deposit ..	2,171.48
Time certs. of deposit	201,862.80
Due to other banks (deposits)	4,591.48
Total deposits	$456,849.17
Capital stock paid in	40,000.00
Surplus	10,000.00
Undivided profits, less expenses, interest and taxes paid	2,540.14
Reserved for depreciation ..	2,166.30
Bills payable, including obligations representing money borrowed	50,000.00
Re-discounts	24,500.00
Total	$586,055.61

MOSCOW

FIRST TRUST & SAVINGS BANK

H. Melgard .... President
M. E. Lewis .... Vice-Pres.
A. Melgard .... 2d Vice-Pres.
W. E. Cahill .... Cashier
W. K. Armour .... Asst. Cashier

Directors—H. Melgard, M. E. Lewis, A. Melgard, W. E. Cahill, S. Barghoorn.

Statement November 15th, 1920.

RESOURCES

Cash on hand ....$	24,044.12
Due from banks	92,642.09
Checks and drafts on other banks	1,405.42
Other cash items	423.00
Loans and discounts	1,096,723.64
Overdrafts	28,340.64
Stocks, bonds, warrants	170,845.06
Banking house, furniture and fixtures	82,693.20
Other real estate	500.00
Total	$1,497,617.17

LIABILITIES

Individual deposits subject to check	$554,975.65
Savings deposits	456,755.23
Postal savings deposits	825.22
Time certs. of deposit	236,507.14
Cashier's checks	9,546.17
Certified checks	83.00
Due to other banks (deposits	12,306.93
Total deposits	1,270,999.34
Capital stock paid in	100,000.00
Surplus	6,000.00
Undivided profits, less expenses, interest and taxes paid	20,413.01
Bills Payable, including obligations representing money borrowed	100,000.00
Other liabilities	204.82
Total	$1,497,617.17

MOSCOW

MOSCOW STATE BANK

Robert Whittier .... Vice-President
Harry Whittier .... Cashier
Chas. N. Lussier .... Asst. Cashier

Directors—Robert Whittier, Harry Whitties, S. L. Willis, C. B. Green, Chas. N. Lussier.

Statement November 15th, 1920.

RESOURCES

Cash on hand ....$	10,594.55
Due from banks	28,017.23
Checks and drafts on other banks	4,976.01
Other cash items	5,849.95
Loans and discounts	620,494.16
Overdrafts	2,598.23
Stocks, bonds, warrants	103,698.35
Banking house, furniture and fixtures	3,330.00
Other real estate	6,600.00
Total ....$	786,158.48

LIABILITIES

Individual deposits subject to check ....$	349,309.87
Savings deposits	230,245.31
Time certs. of deposit	69,756.46
Cashier's checks	5,095.63
Total deposits	654,407.27
Capital stock paid in	25,000.00
Surplus	10,000.00
Undivided profits, less expenses, interest and taxes paid	8,151.21
Bills Payable, including obligations representing money borrowed	88,600.00
Total ....$	786,158.48

MURTAUGH

BANK OF MURTAUGH

C. M. Oberholzer .... President
G. A. Dillon .... Vice-Pres.
T. D. Nash .... Cashier

Directors—C. M. Oberholzer, C. A. Dillon, T. D. Nash, A. J. Fuller, Hyrum Pickett.

Statement November 15th, 1920.

RESOURCES

Cash on hand ....$	2,197.14
Due from banks	17,505.34
Other cash items	26.00
Loans and discounts	98,014.46
Overdrafts	324.09
Stocks, bonds, warrants	10,230.65
Banking house, furniture and fixtures	2,883.49
Other resources	6.98
Total ....$	131,188.15

LIABILITIES

Individual deposits subject to check	55,528.22
Demand certs. of deposit ..	2,500.00
Time certs. of deposit	26,820.25
Cashier's checks	24.73
Total deposits ....$	84,973.20
Capital stock paid in	25,000.00
Surplus	3,500.00
Undivided profits, less expenses, interest and taxes paid	3,075.39
Bills Payable, including obligations representing money borrowed	5,900.00
Re-discounts	8,739.56
Total ....$	131,188.15

NEW MEADOWS

MEADOWS VALLEY BANK

E. J. Osborn .... President
Geo. S. Mitchell .... Vice-Pres.
E. F. Kimbrough .... Cashier
Lee Highley .... Asst. Cashier

Directors—E. J. Osborn, Geo. S.
Mitchell, E. F. Kimbrough, A. R.
Krigbaum.

Statement November 15th, 1920.

RESOURCES

Cash on hand ....$	4,394.20
Due from banks	9,695.68
Other cash items	23.55
Loans and discounts	160,626.41
Stocks, bonds, warrants	2,043.01
Claims, judgments, etc.	2,000.00
Banking house, furniture and fixtures	11,000.00
Other real estate	1,772.59
Other resources	56.30
Total	$191,611.74

LIABILITIES

Individual deposits subject to check	$126,183.66
Demand certs. of deposit ..	403.00
Time certs. of deposit	34,613.91
Total deposits	161,200.57
Capital stock paid in	25,000.00
Surplus	2,750.00
Undivided profits, less expenses, interest and taxes paid	2,661.17
Total	$191,611.74

NEW PLYMOUTH

FARMERS STATE BANK

G. W. Mason .... President
Ross P. Mason .... Cashier
Jessie Campbell .... Asst. Cashier

Directors—G. W. Mason, Ross P.
Mason, John B. Fisher, Walter Burke,
C. M. McBride, Louis Wachter.

Statement November 15th, 1920.

RESOURCES

Cash on hand ....$	4,647.73
Due from banks	5,564.85
Other cash items	3,836.55
Loans and discounts	284,703.18
Stocks, bonds, warrants	1,462.86
Furniture and fixtures	3,000.00
Other real estate	4,370.06
Liberty Loan Bonds	35,673.67
Total	$343,258.90

LIABILITIES

Individual deposits subject to check	197,186.79
Time certs. of deposit	115,828.09
Total deposits ....$	313,015.08
Capital stock paid in	25,000.00
Surplus	5,000.00
Undivided profits, less expenses, interest and taxes	243.82
Total	$343,258.90

NEZPERCE

FARMERS STATE BANK

L. N. Swift .... President
F. F. Johnson .... Vice-Pres.
C. W. Kettman .... Cashier

Directors—L. N. Swift, F. F. Johnson, C. W. Kettman, J. R. Mochler, C. W. Feer.

Statement November 15th, 1920.

RESOURCES

Cash on hand	$ 6,300.38
Due from banks	15,865.32
Checks and drafts on other banks	102.00
Other cash items	129.06
Loans and discounts	201,611.24
Overdrafts	183.07
Stocks, bonds, warrants	10,580.25
Claims, judgments, etc.	2,999.73
Banking house, furniture and fixtures	8,397.53
Other real estate	7,529.30
Total	$253,697.88

LIABILITIES

Individual deposits subject to check	$128,157.60
Savings deposits	6,097.39
Demand certs. of deposit	1,490.07
Time certs. of deposit	68,663.79
Total deposits	204,408.85
Capital stock paid in	35,000.00
Surplus	14,289.03
Total	$253,697.88

NEZPERCE

UNION STATE BANK

C. W. Booth .... President
J. R. Dunham .... Vice-Pres.
Ernst Wienss .... Cashier
C. W. Palmer .... Asst. Cashier

Directors—C. W. Booth, J. R. Dunham, Ernst Wienss, A. F. Harbke, W. F. Johnson, I. H. Jorgens, K. G. Osterhout, Chas. F. Thomas, E. H. Waters.

Statement November 15th, 1920.

RESOURCES

Cash on hand	$ 8,461.09
Due from banks	22,107.25
Checks and drafts on other banks	1,454.69
Loans and discounts	466,730.25
Overdrafts	557.24
Stocks, bonds, warrants	60,054.93
Banking house, furniture and fixtures	31,841.93
Total	$591,207.38

LIABILITIES

Individual deposits subject to check	151,718.78
Savings deposits	96,625.45
Demand certs. of deposit	4,136.41
Time certs. of deposit	38,150.36
Dividends unpaid	35.00
Total deposits	290,666.00
Capital stock paid in	50,000.00
Surplus	10,000.00
Undivided profits, less expenses, interest and taxes paid	6,419.02
Bills Payable, including obligations representing money borrowed	37,000.00
Re-discounts	148,997.36
Customers' Liberty Bond accounts	48,125.00
Total	$591,207.38

OAKLEY

FARMERS COMMERCIAL AND SAVINGS BANK

John McMurray .... President
W. H. Poulton ....Vice-Pres.
J. S. Hanzel .... Cashier
Byron Howell .... Asst. Cashier

Directors—H. R. Matthews, S. P. Worthington, L. E. Bronson, Oscar Iverson, Ray Bedke, John McMurray, W. H. Poulton.

Statement November 15th, 1920.

RESOURCES

Cash on hand ....$	2,799.83
Due from banks	24,787.73
Checks and drafts on other banks	961.57
Other cash items	210.00
Loans and discounts	242,698.77
Overdrafts	862.52
Stocks, bonds, warrants	21,506.68
Banking house, furniture and fixtures	11,126.55
U. S. Bonds, Customers'	12,450.00
Items in transit	1,233.38
Total ....$	318,637.03

LIABILITIES

Individual deposits subject to check ....$	83,946.23
Savings deposits	15,758.39
Time certs. of deposit	56,359.26
Cashier's checks	3,689.30
Total deposits	159,753.18
Capital stock paid in	25,000.00
Surplus	15,000.00
Undivided profits, less expenses, interest and taxes paid	4,167.89
Bills Payable, including obligations representing money borrowed	47,058.85
Re-discounts	54,500.00
Other liabilities—U. S. bonds borrowed	12,450.00
Reserve Fund, bond depreciation	707.11
Total ....$	318,637.03

OAKLEY

OAKLEY STATE BANK

Adam Patterson ....President
L. A. Critchfield ....Vice President
J. D. Cronan ....Cashier
S. A. Laurence ....Asst. Cashier
Amelia Matthews ....Asst. Cashier

Directors—Adam Patterson, L. A. Critchfield, J. D. Cronan, F. C. Bedke, W. R. Gray, Alvin Erickson, Chas. L. Haight, James F. Walker.

Statement November 15th, 1920.

RESOURCES

Cash on hand ....$	2,056.53
Due from banks	19,205.57
Checks and drafts on other banks	3,438.10
Other cash items	2,354.17
Loans and discounts	240,115.98
Stocks, bonds & warrants	4,845.79
Claims, judgments, etc.	1,043.08
Banking house, furniture and fixtures	20,500.00
Other real estate	16,500.00
Other resources	6,787.06
Cash collection account......	572.65
Total ....$	317,418.93

LIABILITIES

Individual deposits subject to check ....$	104,396.47
Savings deposits	28,696.69
Demand certificates of deposit	500.00
Time certificates of deposit	26,489.34
Cashier's checks	8,336.43
Total deposits	168,418.93
Capital stock paid in	25,000.00
Surplus	9,000.00
Bills Payable, including obligations representing money borrowed	115,000.00
Total ....$	317,418.93

OROFINO

BANK OF OROFINO

W. C. Morrow .... President
W. B. Kinne .... Vice-Pres.
C. H. Ede .... Cashier
R. W. Merrill .... Asst. Cashier
E. A. Randall .... Asst. Cashier

Directors—W. C. Morrow, W. B. Kinne, C. H. Ede, Samson Snyder, Theo Fahl.

Statement November 15th, 1920.

RESOURCES

Cash on hand .... $	1,792.42
Due from banks	23,461.30
Checks and drafts on other banks	117.69
Other cash items — None	
Loans and discounts	422,116.54
Overdrafts	1,239.05
Stocks, bonds, warrants	14,955.15
Prem. on bonds—none.	
Acceptances	6,834.07
Banking house, furniture and fixtures	3,690.95
Other real estate	8,498.30
Other resources L. L. Bonds and Transit Acct.	18,489.56
Stock Fed. Reserve Bank ..	900.00
Total ....$	502,095.03

LIABILITIES

Individual deposits subject to check	204,519.78
Savings deposits	51,866.03
Demand certs. of deposit ..	6,154.20
Time certs. of deposit	121,941.73
Total deposits	384,481.74
Capital stock paid in	25,000.00
Surplus	5,000.00
Undivided profits, less expenses, interest and taxes paid	6,425.22
Bills payable, including obligations representing money borrowed	79,000.00
Re-discounts	2,188.07
Total ....$	502,095.03

OROFINO

FIDELITY STATE BANK

Geo. H. Waterman .... President
J. M. Fairly .... Vice-Pres.
Benj. R. Schmid .... Cashier
E. J. Phillips .... Asst. Cashier

Directors—Geo. H. Waterman, J. M. Fairly, Benj. R. Schmid, F. E. Quist, W. A. Waterman.

Statement November 15th, 1920.

RESOURCES

Cash on hand ....$	5,231.25
Due from banks	24,089.78
Checks and drafts on other banks	227.29
Loans and discounts	222,527.46
Overdrafts	303.23
Stocks, bonds. warrants	9,236.32
Claims, judgments, etc.	96.99
Banking house, furniture and fixtures	5,295.00
Total ....$	267,007.32

LIABILITIES

Individual deposits subject to check ....$	115,369.93
Savings deposits	19,172.03
Demand certs. of deposit ..	3,400.54
Time certs. of deposit	64,510.05
Total deposits ....$	202,452.55
Capital stock paid in	10,000.00
Surplus	5,000.00
Undivided profits, less expenses, interest and taxes paid	4,554.77
Bills payable, including obligations representing money borrowed	45,000.00
Total ....$	267,007.32

PARIS

BEAR LAKE STATE BANK

J. R. Shepherd .... President
Wm. L. Rich .... Vice-Pres.
Alfred Budge .... Vice-Pres.
Russell Shepherd .... Cashier

Directors—J. R. Shepherd, Wm. L.
Rich, Alfred Budge, Alma Findlay,
Sam'l Matthews; E. J. Howell, E. M.
Pugmire.

Statement November 15, 1920

RESOURCES

Cash on hand ....$ 16,213.22
Due from banks 51,152.10
Loans and discounts 350,783.07
Stocks, bonds, warrants 9,578.11
Banking house, furniture
 and fixtures 15,163.96

Total $442,890.46

LIABILITIES

Individual deposits subject
 to check $172,929.76
Time certs. of deposit 174,267.72
Cashier's checks 1,670.67

Total deposits 348,868.15
Capital stock paid in 25,000.00
Surplus 10,000.00
Undivided profits, less ex-
 penses, interest and
 taxes paid 7,122.31
Bills payable, including
 obligations representing
 money borrowed 18,000.00
Re-discounts 33,900.00

Total $442,890.46

PAUL

PAUL STATE BANK

Carl Titus .... President
M .E. Watson .... Vice-Pres.
H. N. Yerkes .... Cashier

Directors—Carl Titus, M. E. Watson, H. N. Yerkes, W. C. Larsen, E.
F. Fulkerson, Wm. Treiber.

Statement November 15, 1920

RESOURCES

Cash on hand ....$ 4,894.01
Due from banks 19,530.73
Checks and drafts on
 other banks 949.42
Loans and discounts 122,640.77
Stocks, bonds, warrants 5,757.03
Banking house, furniture
 and fixtures 12,400.00

Total $166,171.96

LIABILITIES

Individual deposits subject
 to check ....$ 78,751.73
Time certs. of deposit 40,708.79
Cashier's checks 7,251.18

Total deposits 126,711.70
Capital stock paid in ....$ 20,000.00
Surplus 2,000.00
Undivided profits, less expenses, interest and
 taxes paid 2,460.26
Bills payable, including
 obligations representing
 money borrowed 15,000.00

Total $166,171.96

PECK

STATE BANK OF PECK.

Geo. H. Waterman .... President
F. E. Quist .... Vice-Pres.
J. A. Haggenmiller .... Cashier
Bertha Chase .... Asst. Cashier

Directors—Geo. H. Waterman, F. E. Quist, J. A. Haggenmiller, W. A. Waterman, E. E. Waterman.

Statement November 15, 1920

RESOURCES

Cash on hand ....$	3,989.85
Due from banks	11,035.80
Other cash items	600.03
Loans and discounts	106,278.10
Overdrafts	428.92
Stocks, bonds, warrants	600.00
Banking house and furn. ..	6,746.06
Other real estate	1,075.33
Total ....$	130,754.09

LIABILITIES

Individual deposits subject to check	53,796.14
Savings deposits	262.96
Time certs. of deposit	39,826.38
Cashier's checks	1,246.49
Due to other banks (deposits)	7,410.38
Total deposits ....$	102,542.35
Capital stock paid in	10,000.00
Surplus	2,500.00
Undivided profits, less expenses, interest and taxes paid	711.74
Bills payable, including obligations representing money borrowed	15,000.00
Total ....$	130,754.09

PICABO

PICABO STATE BANK.

S. L. Reece .... President
Frank Grice .... Vice-Pres.
H. H. Neal .... Cashier

Directors—S. L. Reece, Frank Grice, H. H. Neal, Edw. Cameron, Wm. Black, Jas. Laidlow, Chas. Mc-Glochlin, J. C. Gillihan, Wm. H. Kirkpatrick.

Statement November 15, 1920

RESOURCES

Cash on hand ....$	3,385.08
Due from banks	29,169.09
Checks and drafts on other banks	3,419.29
Loans and discounts	156,106.07
Stocks, bonds, warrants	19,500.99
Claims, judgments, etc.	3,500.00
Banking house, furniture and fixtures	11,700.00
Total ....$	226,780.52

LIABILITIES

Individual deposits subject to check ....$	86,651.92
Savings deposits	4,191.13
Time certs. of deposit	37,305.73
Cashier's checks	1,672.44
Due to other banks (deposits)	954.77
Total deposits ....$	130,775.99
Capital stock paid in	25,000.00
Surplus	5,000.00
Undivided profits, less expenses, interest and taxes paid	3,660.61
Bills payable, including obligations representing money borrowed	39,000.00
Re-discounts	23,343.92
Total ....$	226,780.52

PLUMMER

STATE BANK OF PLUMMER

E. T. Coman .... President
L. F. Connolly .... Vice-Pres.
C. M. Kraemer .... Cashier

Directors—E. T. Coman, L. F. Connolly, C. M. Kraemer, J. N. Wilson.

Statement November 15, 1920

RESOURCES

Cash on hand ....$	5,145.26
Due from banks	13,490.97
Loans and discounts	82,398.56
Stocks, bonds, warrants	39,720.44
Premium on bonds	237.04
Claims, judgments, etc.	363.27
Banking house, furniture and fixtures	4,111.44
Other real estate	1,400.04
Total $146,867.02	

LIABILITIES

Individual deposits subject to check ....$	75,473.38
Savings deposits	25,363.08
Time certs. of deposit	13,615.96
Cashier's checks	2,602.48
Dividends unpaid	300.00
Total deposits $117,354.90	
Capital stock paid in	10,000.00
Surplus	2,000.00
Undivided profits, less expenses, interest and taxes paid	375.08
Other liabilities: Bonds sold with agreement to repurchase	12,237.04
Bonds borrowed	4,900.00
Total $146,867.02	

POCATELLO

CITIZENS BANK

I. N. Anthes .... President
A. B. Bean .... Vice-Pres.
Geo. A. Green .... Vice-Pres.
C. W. Gillies .... Asst. Cashier
W. J. Harvey .... Secretary

Directors—I. N. Anthes, A. B. Bean Geo. A. Greene, W. J. Harvey, W. McCarty.

Statement November 15, 1920

RESOURCES

Cash on hand ....$	4,799.60
Due from banks	112,978.29
Checks and drafts on other banks	18,834.18
Other cash items	43,722.52
Loans and discounts 1,652,696.58	
Overdrafts—None.	
Stocks, bonds, warrants	140,584.42
Claims, judgments, etc	318.52
Banking house, furniture and fixtures	11,165.20
Stock in Fed. Reserve bank	10,800.00
Total $1,995,899.31	

LIABILITIES

Individual deposits subject to check ....$	652,058.06
Savings deposits	200,551.34
Demand certs. of deposit ..	23,350.54
Time certs. of deposit	60,670.55
Certified checks	1.00
Due to other banks (deposits)	32,209.35
Dividends unpaid	126.00
Total deposits 968,766.84	
Capital stock paid in	300,000.00
Surplus	60,000.00
Undivided profits, less expenses, interest and taxes paid	8,775.82
Bills payable, including obligations representing money borrowed	242,500.00
Re-discounts	380,106.65
Bonds borrowed	35,750.00
Total $1,995,899.31	

POCATELLO

FIRST SAVINGS BANK

C. A. Valentine .... President
E. E. Byer .... Vice-Pres.
W. D. Service .... Cashier
P. M. Bryan .... Asst. Cashier

Directors—J. O. Morgan, W. B. Wright, C. A. Valentine, E. E. Byer, W. D. Service.

Statement November 15, 1920

RESOURCES

Cash on hand ....$ 7,621.06
Due from banks 9,591.05
Other cash items 437.97
Loans and discounts 293,969.56
Stocks, bonds, warrants 32,855.74
Banking house, furniture
  and fixtures 2,750.00
Other real estate 24,950.27

Total $372,075.65

LIABILITIES

Individual deposits subject
  to check $115,081.87
Savings deposits 183,523.46
Demand certs. of deposit .. 271.35
Time certs. of deposit 5,429.99
Cashier's checks 656.00

Total deposits 304,962.67
Capital stock paid in 25,000.00
Surplus 25,000.00
Undivided profits, less expenses, interest and
  taxes paid 11,412.98
Bills payable, including
  obligations representing
  money borrowed 5,700.00

Total $372,075.65

POST FALLS

THE VALLEY STATE BANK, LTD.

J. B. Peterson .... President
L. D. Means .... Vice-Pres.
E. R. Anderson .... Vice-Pres.
C. E. Loan .... Cashier

Directors—J. B. Peterson, L. D. Means, E. R. Anderson, C. E. Loan, Mrs. Jno. Richards.

Statement November 15, 1920

RESOURCES

Cash on hand ....$ 7,002.38
Due from banks 20,276.59
Other cash items 104.68
Loans and discounts 136,468.25
Overdrafts 405.72
Stocks, bonds, warrants 8,109.87
Banking house, furniture
  and fixtures 4,500.00
Other real estate 715.00
Liberty Bonds and Certs.
  of Indebtedness 19,800.00
War Savings and Revenue Stamps 47.82

Total $197,430.31

LIABILITIES

Individual deposits subject
  to check $126,188.87
Savings deposits 17,413.78
Time certs. of deposit 35,195.33

Total deposits $178,797.98
Capital stock paid in 10,000.00
Surplus 4,000.00
Undivided profits, less expenses, interest and
  taxes paid 4,632.33

Total $197,430.31

POTLATCH

POTLATCH STATE BANK

A. W. Laird .... President
J. Kendall .... Vice-Pres.
J. H. Bottjer .... Cashier

Directors—A. W. Laird, J. Kendall, J. H. Bottjer, C. A. Weyerhauser, C. R. Musser.

Statement November 15, 1920

RESOURCES

Cash on hand ....$	25,657.86
Due from banks	562,257.87
Checks and drafts on other banks	4,234.10
Other cash items	9,191.27
Loans and discounts	531,985.77
Overdrafts	748.48
Stocks, bonds, warrants	136,871.74
Other real estate	500.00
Banking house, furniture and fixtures	1,630.00
Other resources, Stock in Federal Reserve Bank	1,800.00
Deposit on bonds	2,000.00
Total $1,276,877.09	

LIABILITIES

Individual deposits subject to check $892,088.65	
Savings deposits	136,007.67
Demand certs. of deposit ..	174,304.72
Total deposits $1,202,401.04	
Capital stock paid in	50,000.00
Surplus	10,000.00
Undivided profits, less expenses, interest and taxes paid	13,147.82
Reserved for taxes	1,328.23
Total $1,276,877.09	

PRESTON

IDAHO STATE AND SAVINGS BANK

Ezra C. Foss .... President
Nephi Larsen .... Vice President
Geo. H. Blood .... Cashier
Melvin J. Bishop .... Asst. Cashier

Directors—Ezra C. Foss, Nephi Larsen, G. H. Blood, Calvin J. Foss, James Johnson.

Statement November 15, 1920 ·

RESOURCES

Cash on hand ....$	11,063.47
Due from banks	20,494.81
Checks and drafts on other banks	17,188.12
Loans and discounts	391,368.56
Stocks, bonds & warrants	29,204.26
Claims, judgments, etc	200.00
Banking house, furniture and fixtures	12,147.70
Other real estate	12,682.62
Total $494,349.54	

LIABILITIES

Individual deposits subject to check $209,964.26	
Savings deposits	63,643.58
Time certificates of deposit	48,392.54
Cashier's checks	5,145.60
Certified checks	30.00
Dividends unpaid	1,250.00
Total deposits	328,425.98
Capital stock paid in	50,000.00
Undivided profits, less expenses, interest and taxes paid	3,357.59
Reserved for taxes	3,293.17
Bills payable, including obligations representing money borrowed	97,635.00
Set aside for bank repairs	798.22
Reserve fund for Liberty bonds	88.90
Bond deposits	10,750.68
Total $494,349.54	

PRIEST RIVER

CITIZENS STATE BANK

J. R. Hagman ....President
Agnes Furst ....Vice President
L. E. Van Winkle ....Cashier

Directors—J. R. Hagman, Agnes Furst, L. E. Van Winkle, C. W. Beardmore, W. B. Dingle, Luch Gumaer.

Statement November 15, 1920

RESOURCES

Cash on hand ....$	5,029.18
Due from banks	32,637.36
Checks and drafts on other banks	507.79
Other cash items	700.57
Loans and discounts	171,824.38
Overdrafts	31.31
Stocks, bonds & warrants	19,427.42
Banking house, furniture and fixtures	6,682.65
Other real estate	1,800.40
Total $238,641.06	

LIABILITIES

Individual deposits subject to check $129,350.78	
Savings deposits	69,260.41
Time certificates of deposit	16,130.00
Certified checks	5,017.00
Total deposits	219,758.19
Capital stock paid in	10,000.00
Surplus	5,000.00
Undivided profits, less expenses, interest and taxes paid	3,882.87
Total $238,641.06	

RATHDRUM

RATHDRUM STATE BANK, LTD.

Stewart Young .... President
Frank Wenz ....Vice President
R. E. Young ....Cashier
L. L. Mitchell ....Asst. Cashier

Directors—Stewart Young, Frank Wenz, R. E. Young, J. C. White, A. Cook.

Statement November 15, 1920

RESOURCES

Cash on hand ....$	8,383.19
Due from banks	72,913.18
Loans and discounts	169,331.95
Overdrafts	8.97
Stocks, bonds & warrants	21,982.54
Banking house, furniture and fixtures	16,501.93
Other real estate	7,776.60
Total $296,898.36	

LIABILITIES

Individual deposits subject to check $157,952.66	
Savings deposits	74,538.67
Demand certificates of deposit	22,922.79
Cashier's checks	139.69
Certified checks	12.17
Total deposits	255,566.98
Capital stock paid in	25,000.00
Surplus fund	10,000.00
Undivided profits, less expenses, interest and taxes paid	6,331.38
Total $296,898.36	

REUBENS

BANK OF REUBENS
Private Bank

W. O. Persons ....Cashier

Statement November 15, 1920

RESOURCES

Cash on hand ....$	3,060.54
Due from banks	10,736.13
Checks and drafts on other banks	171.64
Loans and discounts	123,942.59
Overdrafts	2,057.89
Stocks, bonds & warrants	28,129.30
Banking house, furniture and fixtures	1,980.00
Total $170,075.09	

LIABILITIES

Individual deposits subject to check ....$	67,564.46
Demand certificates of deposit	478.18
Time certificates of deposit	43,794.67
Cashier's checks	1,136.43
Total deposits	112,973.74
Capital stock paid in	10,000.00
Surplus	2,000.00
Undivided profits, less expenses, interest and taxes paid	3,401.35
Bills payable, including obligations representing money borrowed	20,000.00
U. S. bond certificates of deposit	21,700.00
Total $170,075.09	

REXBURG

FARMERS & MERCHANTS BANK

Alfred Ricks .... President
J. W. Webster ....Vice President
Nathan Ricks ....Vice President
A. M. Carter ....Vice President
W. E. Gee ....Cashier
J. P. Evans ....Asst. Cashier

Directors—Alfred Ricks, J. W. Webster, Nathan Ricks, A. M. Carter, W. E. Gee, Ephriam Ricks, F. S. Parkinson, A. P. Hamilton, John Taylor, Mark Austin, Peter Taylor, J. S. Webster.

Statement November 15, 1920

RESOURCES

Cash on hand ....$	9,898.38
Due from banks	137,411.41
Checks and drafts on other banks	3,234.07
Other cash items	4.00
Loans and discounts	405,104.66
Overdrafts	None
Stocks, bonds & warrants	126,608.52
Banking house, furniture and fixtures	5,271.50
Expenses in excess of earnings	3,913.34
Total $691,445.88	

LIABILITIES

Individual deposits subject to check ....$	246,996.49
Savings deposits	11,544.56
Time certificates of deposit	40,706.38
Cashier's checks	3,806.00
Total deposits	303,053.43
Capital stock paid in	50,000.00
Surplus	10,000.00
Bills payable, including obligations representing money borrowed	102,610.37
Re-discounts	225,782.08
Total $691,445.88	

REXBURG

REXBURG STATE BANK

R. S. Hunt ....President
J. E. Cosgriff ....Vice President
Jas. R. Wright ....Cashier
H. N. Wright ....Asst. Cashier

Directors—R. S. Hunt, J. E. Cosgriff, Jas. R. Wright, M. Hillman, R. H. Smith.

Statement November 15, 1920

RESOURCES
Cash on hand ....$	12,207.05
Due from banks	63,420.87
Checks and drafts on other banks	5,801.55
Other cash items	9,938.89
Loans and discounts	524.118.74
Overdrafts	668.11
Stocks, bonds & warrants	6,233.54
Banking house, furniture and fixtures	22,321.59
Total ....$	$644,710.34

LIABILITIES
Individual deposits subject to check	$212,792.45
Savings deposits	54,147.76
Time certificates of deposit	20,158.83
Cashier's checks	40,953.66
Certified checks	1.66
Due to other banks (deposits)	10,000.00
Total deposits	338,054.36
Capital stock paid in	40,000.00
Surplus	40,000.00
Undivided profits, less expenses, interest and taxes paid	7,028.82
Bills payable, including obligations representing money borrowed	20,000.00
Re-discounts	199,627.16
Total	$644,710.34

RICHFIELD

FIRST STATE BANK

E. E. Strutz ....President
W. J. Tapper ....Vice President
Geo. R. Schwaner ....Cashier
C. W. Adair ....Asst. Cashier

Directors—E. W. Schwaner, R. J. Lemmon, E. E. Strutz, W. J. Tapper, Geo. R. Schwaner.

Statement November 15, 1920

RESOURCES
Cash on hand ....$	6,940.23
Due from other banks	34,592.42
Checks and drafts on other banks	624.77
Other cash items	187.85
Loans and discounts	100,795.51
Overdrafts	274.40
Stocks, bonds & warrants	46,077.20
Banking house, furniture and fixtures	12,000.00
Other resources, acceptance account customers liability	1,156.75
Total ....$	$202,649.13

LIABILITIES
Individual deposits subject to check	$124,874.76
Savings deposits	11,070.81
Demand certificates of deposit	3.65
Time certificates of deposit	23,086.56
Cashier's checks	733.50
Total deposits	159,769.28
Capital stock paid in	25,000.00
Surplus	4,000.00
Undivided profits, less expenses, interest and taxes paid	1,901.11
Reserved for taxes	421.50
Bills payable, including obligations representing money borrowed	10,000.00
Other liabilities, Liberty bond depreciation res.	1,557.24
Total	$202,649.13

RIGBY

ANDERSON BROS. BANK

Jas. E. Steele ....President
Geo. A. Condon ....Vice President
L. A. Foster ....Asst. Cashier

Directors—Jas. E. Steele, Geo. A. Condon, M. M. Hitt, A. C. Cordon.

Statement November 15, 1920

RESOURCES

Cash on hand	$ 8,804.30
Due from banks	20,576.70
Checks and drafts on other banks	5,628.90
Other cash items	107.02
Loans and discounts	161,596.29
Overdrafts	None
Stocks, bonds, warrants	57,542.79
Banking house, furniture and fixtures	1,000.00
Other real estate	700.00
Total	$255,956.00

LIABILITIES

Individual deposits subject to check	$127,576.56
Savings deposits	1,289.26
Time certificates of deposit	71,238.46
Cashier's checks	2,539.96
Due to other banks (deposits)	1,461.54
Total deposits	204,105.78
Capital stock paid in	10,000.00
Surplus	10,000.00
Undivided profits, less expenses, interest and taxes paid	6,850.22
Bills payable, including obligations representing money borrowed	25,000.00
Total	$255,956.00

ROBERTS

BANK OF ROBERTS

C. A. Spath ....President
O. K. Wilbur ....Vice President
W. A. Davis ....Cashier

Directors—C. A. Spath, O. K. Wilbur, W. A. Davis, C. L. Harwood, Otto E. McCutcheon.

Statement, November 15, 1920

RESOURCES

Cash on hand	$ 3,094.48
Due from banks	12,175.98
Other cash items	625.05
Loans and discounts	129,497.81
Stocks, bonds & warrants	7,693.34
Banking house, furniture and fixtures	3,250.00
Other resources, U. S. Liberty bonds and Thrift stamps	89.25
Total	$156,465.91

LIABILITIES

Individual deposits subject to check	$ 78,555.46
Time certificates of deposit	17,428.85
Cashier's checks	3,050.00
Total deposits	99,034.31
Capital stock paid in	25,000.00
Surplus	3,500.00
Undivided profits, less expenses, interest and taxes paid	1,663.49
Re-discounts	27,248.11
Savings banks sold	20.00
Total	$156,465.91

ROCKLAND

FIRST STATE BANK

J. T. Fisher .... President
H. P. Houtz .... Vice President
James E. Ogden ....Cashier

Directors—J. T. Fisher, H. P. Houtz, James E. Ogden, S. N. Morris, E. N. Morris.

Statement, November 15, 1920

RESOURCES

Cash on hand ....$	2,298.47
Due from banks	21,103.60
Checks and drafts on other banks	782.11
Loans and discounts	87,652.44
Overdrafts	1,730.30
Stocks, bonds & warrants	2,242.74
Banking house, furniture and fixtures	6,000.00
Expenses in excess of earnings	115.39
Total ....$	123,925.05

LIABILITIES

Individual deposits subject to check ....$	72,481.12
Time certificates of deposit	24,630.05
Total deposits	97,111.17
Capital stock paid in..........	10,000.00
Surplus	6,000.00
Bills payable, including obligations representing money borrowed	10,000.00
Other liabilities	813.88
Total ....$	123,925.05

ROGERSON

BANK OF ROGERSON

J. S. Bussell ....President
Louis Harrell ....Vice President
W. M. Hines ....Cashier

Directors—J. S. Bussell, Louis Harrell, W. M. Hines, John McRae, A. Rogerson.

Statement, November 15, 1920

RESOURCES

Cash on hand ....$	8,011.36
Due from banks	48,039.02
Checks and drafts on other banks	266.52
Loans and discounts	235,811.59
Overdrafts	288.49
Banking house, furniture and fixtures	4,000.00
Other real estate	6,739.30
Other resources	3,631.87
Total ....$	306,788.35

LIABILITIES

Individual deposits subject to check ....$	150,998.38
Time certificates of deposit	108,945.61
Cashier's checks	2,103.18
Total deposits	262,047.17
Capital stock paid in	25,000.00
Surplus	10,000.00
Undivided profits, less expenses, interest and taxes paid	9,741.18
Total ....$	306,788.35

RUPERT

FARMERS & MERCHANTS BANK

E. R. Dampier .... President
John Brockie ....Vice President
J. D. Ritchie ....Cashier

Directors—E. R. Dampier, John Brockie, E. L. Rigg, D. R. Pingree, Henry Hite.

Statement, November 15, 1920

RESOURCES
Cash on hand ....$	7,795.67
Due from banks	19,325.47
Checks and drafts on other banks	3,605.29
Other cash items	1,189.60
Loans and discounts	168,513.35
Banking house, furniture and fixtures	4,150.00
Stocks, bonds & warrants	19,305.22
Other real estate	8,469.11
Stock in Federal Reserve Bank	1,050.71
Total ....$	$233,403.71

LIABILITIES
Individual deposits subject to check ....$	47,368.65
Savings deposits	1,097.34
Time certificates of deposit	37,414.25
Cashier's checks	10,657.65
Certified checks	134.30
Total deposits	96,672.19
Capital stock paid in	35,000.00
Undivided profits, less expenses, interest and taxes paid	2,299.88
Bills payable, including obligations representing money borrowed	57,000.00
Re-discounts with Federal Reserve bank	36,631.64
Bills payable Federal Reserve bank, secured by U. S. bonds	5,800.00
Total ....$	$233,403.71

ST. ANTHONY

ST. ANTHONY BANK & TRUST COMPANY

M. J. Gray ....President
Jas. G. Gwinn ....Vice President
L. H. Neal ....Cashier
A. L. Hallstrom ....Asst. Cashier
J. B. Quayle ....Asst. Cashier

Directors—M. J. Gray, Jas. G. Gwinn, L. H. Neal, S. W. Orme, A. D. Miller, Jr., S. L. Reece.

Statement, November 15, 1920

RESOURCES
Cash on hand ....$	7,257.82
Due from banks	38,402.96
Checks and drafts on other banks	24,327.22
Other cash items	886.75
Loans and discounts	574,657.79
Overdrafts	None
Stocks, bonds & warrants	39,452.49
Banking house, furniture and fixtures	9,585.00
Other real estate	324.80
Stock in Federal Reserve bank	1,650.00
Liberty Bonds	54,900.00
Total ....$	$751,444.83

LIABILITIES
Individual deposits subject to check ....$	$263,554.11
Savings deposits	55,366.52
Time certificates of deposit	62,020.53
Cashier's checks	17,543.59
Certified checks	30.00
Due to other banks (deposits)	4,344.24
Total deposits	402,858.99
Capital stock paid in	30,000.00
Surplus	30,000.00
Undivided profits, less expenses, interest and taxes paid	2,938.44
Bills payable, including obligations representing money borrowed	127,500.00
Re-discounts	158,147.40
Total ....$	$751,444.83

ST. JOE

FIRST STATE BANK

R. L. Rutter .... President
W. F. Burkholtz .... Vice-Pres.
E. F. Betz ....Cashier

Directors—R. L. Rutter, W. F. Burkholtz, A. D. Price, A. W. Wendorf, Ella E. Buckholtz, J. P. M. Richards, W. S. McCrae.

Statement, November 15, 1920

RESOURCES

Cash on hand ....$	7,214.12
Due from banks	25,553.36
Loans and discounts	77,779.19
Stocks, bonds & warrants	6,302.40
Banking house, furniture and fixtures	501.00
Total $117,350.07	

LIABILITIES

Individual deposits subject to check ....$	59,108.24
Savings deposits	27,132.49
Time certificates of deposit	13,178.03
Total deposits	99,418.76
Capital stock	10,000.00
Surplus	3,500.00
Undivided profits, less expenses, interest and taxes paid	3,572.87
Reserved for taxes, interest, insurance, etc.	858.44
Total $117,350.07	

ST. MARIES

LUMBERMENS STATE BANK

C. W. Craney .... President
J. G. Fralick .... Vice-Pres.
Court M. Sargent .... Cashier
I. F. Shefler .... Asst. Cashier

Directors—C. W. Craney, J. G. Fralick, Court M. Sargent, H. H. Craney, Geo. O'Dwyer.

Statement, November 15, 1920

RESOURCES

Cash on hand ....$	18,644.04
Due from banks	84,908.08
Checks and drafts on other banks	826.60
Other cash items	1,024.19
Loans and discounts	403,896.34
Stocks, bonds, warrants	170,979.93
Banking house, furniture and fixtures	28,100.00
Other real estate	3,287.16
Other resources	149.29
Total $711,815.63	

LIABILITIES

Individual deposits subject to check $413,872.75	
Savings deposits	126,874.18
Postal Savings deposits	1,722.30
Demand certs. of deposit ..	1,260.00
Time certs. of deposit	69,082.38
Cashier's checks	22,987.09
Certified checks	2.40
Due to other banks (deposits)	6,980.34
Dividends unpaid	114.00
Total deposits $642,895.44	
Capital stock paid in	50,000.00
Surplus	12,500.00
Undivided profits, less expenses, interest and taxes paid	4,196.47
Res. for taxes and interest	500.00
Other liabilities, reserved for depreciation	1,723.72
Total $711,815.63	

SALMON

PIONEER BANK & TRUST CO.

W. C. Shoup .... President
W. W. Slavin .... Vice-Pres.
E. Hill .... Cashier

Directors—W. C. Shoup, W. W. Slavin, E. Hill, David Edson, Thos. Pyeatt, C. H. Rose, W. H. Shoup.

Statement, November 15, 1920

RESOURCES

Cash on hand ....$	9,712.25
Due from banks	36,891.66
Checks and drafts on other banks	1,249.12
Other cash items	310.00
Loans and discounts	395,955.65
Stocks, bonds, warrants	31,724.39
Banking house, furniture and fixtures	3,763.85
Total ....$	479,606.92

LIABILITIES

Individual deposits subject to check ....$	214,519.90
Savings deposits	22,654.39
Demand certs. of deposit ..	1.00
Time certs. of deposit	79,302.20
Cashier's checks	3,177.61
Total deposits ....$	319,655.10
Capital stock paid in	35,000.00
Surplus	30,000.00
Undivided profits, less expenses, interest and taxes paid	4,951.82
Bills payable, including obligations representing money borrowed	90,000.00
Total ....$	479,606.92

SHELLEY

COMMERCIAL BANK

S. L. Reece .... President
J. L. Moore .... Vice-Pres.
W. S. Wright .... Cashier
Goldie White .... Asst. Cashier

Directors—S. L. Reece, J. L. Moore, W. S. Wright, H. L. Malcolm.

Statement, November 15, 1920

RESOURCES

Cash on hand ....$	9,674.54
Due from banks	60,331.57
Checks and drafts on other banks	5,037.37
Other cash items	804.84
Loans and discounts	289,755.00
Overdrafts — None.	
Stocks, bonds, warrants	5,362.21
Banking house, furniture and fixtures	17,000.00
Other resources	536.56
Expenses in excess of earnings	1,924.61
Total ....$	390,426.70

LIABILITIES

Individual deposits subject to check	220,498.01
Savings deposits	43,606.99
Time certs. of deposit	14,359.91
Cashier's checks	9,261.79
Total deposits	287,726.70
Capital stock paid in	20,000.00
Surplus	16,000.00
Bills payable, including obligations representing money borrowed	57,800.00
Re-discounts	8,900.00
Total ....$	390,426.70

SODA SPRINGS

BANK OF SODA SPRINGS

J. E. Lau .... President
J. Geo. Schmidt .... Vice-Pres.
J. T. Torgesen .... Cashier
L. A. Richards .... Asst. Cashier

Directors—J. E. Lau, J. George Schmidt, E. D. Whitman, R. B. Gunnell, Mrs. John Ferebauer.

Statement, November 15, 1920

RESOURCES

Cash on hand ....$ 4,023.64
Due from banks 4,774.71
Checks and drafts on
other banks 728.35
Other cash items 789.46
Loans and discounts 194,091.89
Overdrafts 126.22
Stocks, bonds, warrants 6,545.07
Banking house, furniture
and fixtures 11,369.00

Total $222,448.34

LIABILITIES

Individual deposits subject
to check 107,312.83
Time certs. of deposit 4,740.42
Cashier's checks 2,625.46
Due to other banks (deposits) 313.50

Total deposits 114,992.21
Capital stock paid in 25,000.00
Surplus 10,000.00
Undivided profits, less expenses, interest and
taxes paid 1,033.13
Bills payable, including
obligations representing
money borrowed 4,000.00
Re-discounts 67,423.00

Total $222,448.34

SODA SPRINGS

LARGILLIERE & COMPANY, BANKERS
Private Bank

A. Largilliere .... President
E. W. Largilliere .... Cashier
Jessie E. Moore .... Asst. Cashier

Statement, November 15, 1920

RESOURCES

Cash on hand ....$ 13,036.47
Due from banks 46,864.26
Checks and drafts on
other banks 2,335.60
Loans and discounts 319,223.07
Overdrafts 1,241.22
Stocks, bonds, warrants 30,860.64
Claims, judgments, etc. 1,061.74
Furniture and fixtures 2,257.20

Total $416,880.20

LIABILITIES

Individual deposits subject
to check $260,254.50
Savings deposits 4,242.87
Time certs. of deposit 101,474.17
Cashier's checks 4,360.99

Total deposits $370,332.53
Capital stock paid in 25,000.00
Surplus 12,000.00
Undivided profits, less expenses, interest and
taxes paid 9,547.67
Bills payable, including
obligations representing
money borrowed None.
Re-discounts .... None.

Total $416,880.20

SPIRIT LAKE

BANK OF SPIRIT LAKE

G. F. Hagenbuch .... President
Geo. R. Charters, Jr. .... Vice-Pres.
C. C. Richardson .... Cashier
R. H. Graham .... Asst. Cashier

Directors—G. F. Hagenbuch, Geo. R. Charters, Jr., C. C. Richardson, W. F. Webb, J. K. McCornack.

Statement November 15, 1920

RESOURCES

Cash on hand ....$	8,212.13
Due from banks	9,792.36
Other cash items	240.93
Loans and discounts	219,193.36
Stocks, bonds, warrants	29,446.44
Claims, judgments, etc.	2,964.25
Banking house, furniture and fixtures	15,703.25
Other resources, Revenue stamps	44.86
Total ....$	285,597.58

LIABILITIES

Individual deposits subject to check ....$	144,176.48
Savings deposits	75,148.77
Time certs. of deposit	25,383.37
Cashier's checks	579.29
Due to other banks (deposits)	2,997.84
Total deposits	248,285.75
Capital stock paid in	25,000.00
Surplus	5,000.00
Undivided profits, less expenses, interest and taxes paid	7,311.83
Total ....$	285,597.58

STAR

THE FARMERS BANK

J. W. Jones .... President
Frank Martin .... Vice-Pres.
J. E. Roberts .... Cashier
J. W. Mershon .... Asst. Cashier

Directors—J. W. Jones, Frank Martin, J. E. Roberts, E. E. Lister, G. R. Hitt.

Statement November 15, 1920

RESOURCES

Cash on hand ....$	3,232.40
Due from banks	28,911.53
Checks and drafts on other banks	75.00
Other cash items	32.79
Loans and discounts	179,085.19
Overdrafts	514.00
Stocks, bonds, warrants	3,722.32
Banking house, furniture and fixtures	2,000.00
Other real estate	8,000.00
Stock in Federal Reserve bank	1,050.00
U. S. Liberty Bonds and Treasury Certs.	90,900.00
Total ....$	317,523.23

LIABILITIES

Individual deposits subject to check	146,602.63
Savings deposits	73.65
Demand certs. of deposit ..	7,240.00
Time certs. of deposit	88,760.30
Total deposits	242,676.58
Capital stock	25,000.00
Surplus	10,000.00
Undivided profits	4,662.26
Bills payabue	35,000.00
Reserve for bond depreciation	184.39
Total ....$	317,523.23

STITES

BANK OF STITES

I. Ewing .... President
A. Olson .... Vice-Pres.
F. E. Leeper .... Cashier
Helen Leeper .... Asst. Cashier

Directors—I. Ewing, A. Olson, F. E. Leeper, Amelia Ewing, J. B. Leeper.

Statement November 15, 1920

RESOURCES
Cash on hand ....$	1,178.25
Due from banks	1,714.94
Loans and discounts	53,452.13
Overdrafts	293.20
Stocks, bonds, warrants	359.25
Claims, judgments, etc.	60.00
Banking house, furniture and fixtures	4,000.00
Other real estate	4,494.05
Expenses in excess of earnings	338.36
Total ....$	65,890.18

LIABILITIES
Individual deposits subject to check	22,379.29
Time certs. of deposit	11,660.89
Total deposits	34,040.18
Capital stock paid in	10,000.00
Surplus	2,000.00
Bills payable, including obligations representing money borrowed	19,850.00
Total ....$	65,890.18

SUGAR CITY

FREMONT COUNTY BANK

Mark Austin .... President
G. E. Bowerman .... Vice-Pres.
F. L. Davis .... Cashier
L. A. Davis .... Asst. Cashier

Directors—Mark Austin, G. E. Bowerman, F. L. Davis, R. J. Comstock, J. L. Roberts, Alfred Ricks.

Statement November 15, 1920

RESOURCES
Cash on hand ....$	13,069.83
Due from banks	95,479.55
Checks and drafts on other banks	141.44
Other cash items	82.78
Loans and discounts	253,520.34
Overdrafts—None.	
Stocks, bonds, warrants	1,900.00
Banking house, furniture and fixtures	10,180.00
U. S. Liberty and Victory Bonds	51,250.00
Total ....$	425,623.94

LIABILITIES
Individual deposits subject to check ....$	260,810.70
Savings deposits	20,426.33
Demand certs. of deposit ..	1,786.33
Time certs. of deposit	28,352.42
Cashier's checks	3,995.79
Certified checks	7.50
Due to other banks (deposits)	4,231.59
Total deposits	319,610.66
Capital stock paid in	25,000.00
Surplus	5,000.00
Undivided profits, less expenses, interest and taxes paid	13,263.28
Reserved for taxes	800.00
Bills payable, including obligations representing money borrowed	45,000.00
Re-discounts	2,500.00
Liberty Loan deposits	14,450.00
Total ....$	425,623.94

TETON CITY

FIRST STATE BANK

J. C. Siddoway .... President
J. L. Briggs .... Vice-Pres.
R. C. Berry .... Cashier

Directors—J. C. Siddoway, J. L. Briggs, R. C. Berry, T. M. Thomson, Jacob Johnston, A. J. Siddoway.

Statement November 15, 1920

RESOURCES

Cash on hand ....$	1,728.61
Due from banks	7,849.24
Checks and drafts on other banks	319.27
Other cash items	38.53
Loans and discounts	105,311.68
Stocks, bonds, warrants	7,726.81
Banking house, furniture and fixtures	14,991.06
Stock in Fed. Res. Bank ..	1,000.00
Total ....$	138,965.20

LIABILITIES

Individual deposits subject to check ....$	63,964.76
Savings deposits	2,637.10
Time certs. of deposit	11,356.75
Cashier's checks	920.90
Total deposits	78,879.51
Capital stock paid in	30,000.00
Undivided profits, less expenses, interest and taxes paid	695.48
Bills payable, including obligations representing money borrowed	4,350.00
Re-discounts	25,040.21
Total ....$	138,965.20

TETONIA

FARMERS STATE BANK

C. B. Walker .... President
M. E. Phillips .... Vice-Pres.
C. F. Cawles .... Vice-Pres.
J. H. Jensen .... Cashier

Directors—C. B. Walker, M. E. Phillips, C. F. Cawles, J. H. Jensen, W. W. Taylor, R. C. Kimball, H. S. Egbert, A. C. Miner.

Statement November 15, 1920

RESOURCES

Cash on hand ....$	2,275.31
Due from banks	10,779.97
Loans and discounts	134,391.65
Overdrafts	407.32
Stocks, bonds, warrants	1,253.91
Banking house, furniture and fixtures	11,513.44
Other resources	850.00
Total ....$	161,471.60

LIABILITIES

Individual deposits subject to check	50,737.03
Time certs. of deposit	8,761.18
Cashier's checks	4,329.62
Total deposits	63,827.83
Capital stock paid in	25,000.00
Surplus	2,500.00
Undivided profits, less expenses, interest and taxes paid	733.77
Bills payable, including obligations representing money borrowed	10,000.00
Re-discounts	59,410.00
Total ....$	161,471.60

TROY

FIRST BANK OF TROY

O. Bohman .... President
O. Larson .... Vice-Pres.
C. Larson .... Cashier
G. Poulson .... Asst. Cashier
Directors—O. Bohman, O. Larson, C. Larson, Fred K. Bressler, O. H. Johnson, Axel Bohman, Emil Nelson.

Statement November 15, 1920

RESOURCES

Cash on hand ....$	14,120.77
Due from banks	51,316.00
Checks and drafts on other banks	242.35
Other cash items — None	
Loans and discounts	358,113.79
Overdrafts	1,041.93
Stocks, bonds, warrants	12,425.84
Premium on bonds None.	
Claims, Judg'ts, etc. None	
Banking house, furniture and fixtures	7,750.00
Other real estate	2,250.00
Other resources	343.90
Expenses in excess of earnings — None.	
Total ....$	447,604.58

LIABILITIES

Individual deposits subject to check ....$	177,186.43
Savings deposits—None.	
Postal Sav. deposits—None.	
Demand certs. of deposit ..	192.03
Time certs. of deposit	238,113.27
Cashier's checks	15.00
Certified checks—None	
Due to other banks (deposits)—None.	
Dividends unpaid	650.00
Total deposits	416,156.73
Capital stock paid in	20,000.00
Surplus	10,000.00
Undivided profits, less expenses, interest and taxes paid	1,447.85
Res. for taxes—None.	
Bills payable—None.	
Re-discounts — None	
Other liabilities—None.	
Total ....$	447,604.58

TWIN FALLS

IDAHO STATE BANK

C. J. Hahn .... President
C. N. Beatty .... Vice-Pres.
L. F. Bracken .... Cashier
Ray McClellan .... Asst. Cashier
Directors—C. P. Bowles, C. Fahrney, C. J. Hahn, C. N. Beatty, L. F. Bracken.

Statement November 15, 1920

RESOURCES

Cash on hand ....$	7,550.34
Due from banks	52,140.09
Checks and drafts on other banks	8,913.66
Other cash items	2,361.90
Loans and discounts	380,539.44
Overdrafts	882.28
Stocks, bonds, warrants	40,484.09
Claims, judgments, etc.	128.40
Banking house, furniture and fixtures	18,052.93
Total ....$	511,053.13

LIABILITIES

Individual deposits subject to check	257,376.32
Savings deposits	33,434.69
Time certs. of deposit	75,916.44
Cashier's checks	22,520.60
Certified checks	556.26
Total deposits ....$	389,804.11
Capital stock paid in	50,000.00
Surplus	6,500.00
Undivided profits, less expenses, interest and taxes paid	748.82
Bills payable, including obligations representing money borrowed	64,000.00
Total ....$	511,053.13

TWIN FALLS

TWIN FALLS BANK & TRUST COMPANY

W. S. McCornick .... President
J. S. Bussell .... Vice-Pres.
J. G. Bradley .... Cashier
Curtis Turner .... Asst. Cashier
Directors—H. A. McCornick, L. T. Wright, W. S. McCornick, J. S. Bussell, J. G. Bradley.

Statement November 15, 1920

RESOURCES

Cash on hand ....$	33,901.63
Due from banks	169,143.13
Checks and drafts on other banks	38,723.38
Other cash items	2,401.57
Loans and discounts 1,455,951.81	
Overdrafts	4,882.40
Stocks, bonds, warrants	517,850.87
Claims, judgments, etc.	4,076.31
Banking house, furniture and fixtures	65,108.05
Other real estate	3,651.00
Total $2,290,690.24	

LIABILITIES

Individual deposits subject to check $961,876.12	
Savings deposits	217,501.32
Demand certs. of deposit ..	1,543.20
Time certs. of deposit	232,489.82
Cashier's checks	12,192.30
Certified checks	2,560.71
Due to other banks (deposits)	117,614.65
Total deposits $1,545,778.52	
Capital stock paid in	100,000.00
Surplus	75,000.00
Undivided profits, less expenses, interest and taxes paid	25,780.76
Reserved for taxes	439.14
Bills payable, including obligations representing money borrowed	373,750.00
Re-discounts	169,141.82
Other liabilities, letter of credit	800.00
Total $2,290,690.24	

VICTOR

VICTOR STATE BANK

B. F. Blodgett .... President
R. A. Drake .... Vice-Pres.
Ed. Riggan .... Vice-Pres.
S. M. Meickle .... Cashier
J. D. Lauritzen .... Asst. Cashier
Directors—C. M. Hatch, Nahum Curtis, Ed Riggan, F. J. Stone, W. J. Tonks, B. F. Blodgett, R. A. Drake.

Statement November 15, 1920

RESOURCES

Cash on hand ....$	1,356.75
Due from banks	6,682.39
Loans and discounts	175,603.20
Overdrafts	703.45
Stocks, bonds, warrants	28,441.93
Banking house, furniture and fixtures	19,879.50
Fed. Res. Bank stock	1,000.00
Collections	61.75
Total $233,728.97	

LIABILITIES

Individual deposits subject to check ....$	58,145.67
Demand certs. of deposit ..	49.64
Time certs. of deposit	40,181.85
Other time deposits	6,550.00
Cashier's checks	3,887.61
Due to other banks (deposits)	574.09
Total deposits	109,388.86
Capital stock paid in	25,000.00
Surplus	8,000.00
Undivided profits, less expenses, interest and taxes paid	3,013.77
Bills payable, including obligations representing money borrowed	36,100.00
Re-discounts	52,226.24
Total	233,728.97

WALLACE

WALLACE BANK & TRUST CO.

Jerome J. Day .... President
Ramsey M. Walker .... Vice-Pres.
Paul Leuschel .... Cashier

Directors—Harry L. Day, Jerome
J. Day, Ramsey M. Walker, Paul
Leuschel, F. M. Rothrock, Axel P.
Ramstedt, D. C. McKissick, John P.
Mahoney.

Statement November 15, 1920

RESOURCES

Cash on hand ....\$	492,237.00
Due from banks 1,	416,263.82
Checks and drafts on other banks	2,751.21
Other cash items	6,311.35
Loans and discounts 1,	262,231.36
Stocks, bonds, warrants	875,120.73
Premium on bonds	6,809.16
Claims, judgments, etc.	4,117.62
Banking house, furniture and fixtures	62,171.71
Other resources, War Savings Stamps	1,195.27
Total \$4,	130,209.23

LIABILITIES

Individual deposits subject to check \$3,	087,268.19
Savings deposits	187,127.69
Postal savings deposits	24,750.88
Demand certs. of deposit ..	339.90
Time certs. of deposit	235,685.35
Cashier's checks	30,649.43
Due to other banks (deposits)	244,204.41
Dividends unpaid	1,500.00
Total deposits 3,	811,525.85
Capital stock paid in	100,000.00
Surplus	100,000.00
Undivided profits, less expenses, interest and taxes paid	62,563.21
Other liabilities, reserved for emergencies	56,120.17
Total \$4,	130,209.23

WARDNER

WEBER BANK

J. H. Weber .... President
P. P. Weber .... Vice-Pres.
Thos. R. Jones .... Cashier
A. T. Combs .... Asst. Cashier

Directors—J. H. Weber, P. P. Weber, Thos. R. Jones, A. T. Combs,
Chas. McKinnis.

Statement November 15, 1920

RESOURCES

Cash on hand ....\$	3,962.94
Due from banks	17,490.44
Loans and discounts	86,154.28
Stocks, bonds, warrants	31,725.00
Banking house, furniture and fixtures	800.00
Other real estate	3,680.00
Total ....\$	143,812.66

LIABILITIES

Individual deposits subject to check ....\$	75,264.41
Postal savings deposits	3,598.03
Demand certs. of deposit ..	175.00
Time certs. of deposit	35,738.80
Due to other banks (deposits)	406.01
Total deposits	115,182.25
Capital stock paid in	20,000.00
Surplus	5,000.00
Undivided profits, less expenses, interest and taxes paid	3,630.41
Total ....\$	143,812.66

CPSIA information can be obtained at www.ICGtesting.com
Printed in the USA
LVOW052226151012

302948LV00015BA/75/P